A LIE OF THE MIND

A Play in Three Acts

SAM SHEPARD

The Royal Court Writers Series
published by Methuen
in association with the Royal Court Theatre

ROYAL COURT WRITERS SERIES

First published in Great Britain as a paperback original in 1987
by Methuen London Ltd, 11 New Fetter Lane, London EC4P 4EE
Reprinted in this programme/text edition for the Royal Court Writers Series, 1987

A Lie of the Mind copyright © 1986 by Sam Shepard
Printed in Great Britain by Expression Printers Ltd, London N7 9DP

British Library Cataloguing in Publication Data
Shepard, Sam
    A lie of the mind: a play in three acts.
    ———(A Methuen modern play).
    I. Title
    812'.54   PS3569.H394

    ISBN 01-413-16100-5

THE ROYAL COURT THEATRE CHALLENGE FUND

As the national theatre of new writing it is the Royal Court's particular role to produce challenging new work and maintain British theatre as the most exciting in the world. Once again we have a shortfall in funding that threatens the number of plays we can produce. This year our estimated budget deficit is £93,000. We have to raise at least this amount (more, if we want to fund new or additional developments). Last year, we raised with your help £63,000.

One of the ways in which we hope to raise the target sum is through our Patronage Scheme — aimed at both business and private sources.

• **For £1,000** you can be a Patron, and in return we will offer you four top price tickets for each show Upstairs or Down throughout the year. In addition we will entertain you and your guests before each show and during the interval. You will be given life membership of the Royal Court Theatre Society.

• **For £250** you can become a Sponsor, which entitles you to two top price tickets for a Preview or the First Night of each show Up and Down throughout the year and membership of the Theatre Society for five years.

• **For £50** you can be a Friend of the Royal Court and we will give you two tickets for a Preview of every Main House show throughout the year.

Patrons
Central Independent Television plc, Henny Gestetner.

Sponsors
Linda Bassett; Alan Bennett; Michael Codron; Anne Devlin; David Kleeman; London Arts Discovery Tours; Lesley Manville; Patricia Marmont; Marmont Management; Debbie McWilliams; Jonathan Miller; Alfred Molina; Gary Oldman; Greville Poke; Margaret Ramsay; Sir Dermot de Trafford.

Friends
John Arthur; Glen Berelowitz & Lindsey Stevens; Connie Booth; Jim Broadbent; Paul Brooke; Ralph Brown; Carol Bush; Guy Chapman; Angela Coles; Jeremy Conway; Lou Coulson; Timothy Dalton; Alan David; William and Libby Duffy; Adrian Dunbar; Dolores Edwardes; Jan Evans, Evans & Reiss; John Evans & Judith Fenn; Trevor Eve; Kenneth Ewing, Fraser & Dunlop Scripts Ltd; Peter Eyre; Kate Feast; Rachel Feuchtwang; Gilly Fraser; Ray Freeston, Keith Prowse Ltd; David Gant; Kerry Gardner; Anne Garwood; Jonathan Gems; Paul Hamlyn, Octopus Publishing Group plc; Sharon Hamper, Hamper Neafsey Associates; Jocelyn Herbert; Derek Hornby; David Horovitch; John & Ros Hubbard, Hubbard Casting; Dusty Hughes; Kenny Ireland; J C & M E Jaqua; Paul Jesson; Anthony Jones; Alex King; Sara Lathrop; Sheila Lemon; Mrs C Lush; Suzie Mackenzie; Philip McDonald; Marina Martin; Richard O'Brien; Stephen Oliver; Sophie Sky Okonedu; Harold Pinter; Louise Stein Plaschkes; Mrs M Platton-King; Jane Rayne; Alan Rickman; A J Sayers; Roxanne Shafer; Sir Clive Sinclair; Mrs D Stafford-Clark; Richard Stone; Nigel Terry; Mary Trevelyan; Tracey Ullman; Maureen Vincent, Fraser & Dunlop Ltd; Julian Wadham; Julie Walters; Sarah Wheatland; Richard Wilson

and the Companies of: *Road, Ourselves Alone, Kafka's Dick, Serious Money,*

Financially assisted by the Arts Council of Great Britain, the Royal Borough of Kensington and Chelsea and the London Boroughs Grant Scheme.

Arts Council Funded

COMING NEXT
IN THE MAIN HOUSE 730 1745

From 4 January
The Traverse Theatre production of
MAN TO MAN by Manfred Karge   Translated by Anthony Vivis
Directed by Stephen Unwin

'A German fairy-tale of our time' with a 'devastating' performance by Tilda
Swinton that is 'at once cocky and cheeful, a perfect interpretation'. THE
OBSERVER

IN THE THEATRE UPSTAIRS 730 2554
From 3 November
The National Theatre Education Department tour of
The National Studio production of
APART FROM GEORGE written and directed by Nick Ward

APART FROM GEORGE tells the story of a Fenland family hit by the
redundancy of George, a farm worker, and the household's breadwinner.
With no prospect of other work, George has to deal with the pressures of
losing his self-respect and sense of purpose.
This Fenland tragedy is illuminated by moments of comic and poetic
intensity and contains ensemble acting of rare emotional depth.

From 1 December
A Paines Plough production in association with
the Belgrade Theatre, Coventry of
THE WAY TO GO HOME by Rona Munro
Directed by Pip Broughton

A political thriller set in Turkey. Two Scottish women get involved in a
dangerous game of pursuit, escape and random chance, which brings a
nervous world to the brink of war.

AND AT WYNDHAM'S THEATRE
SERIOUS MONEY by Caryl Churchill
Directed by Max Stafford-Clark

Box Office 836 3028 CC 279 6565/4444 (Open all hours) 741 9999 Groups
836 3962

"Love the City or Hate it, but see this" DAILY TELEGRAPH

A LIE OF THE MIND

BY SAM SHEPARD

CAST IN ORDER OF APPEARANCE

JAKE	WILL PATTON
FRANKIE, *Jake's Brother*	PAUL McGANN
BETH, *Jake's wife*	MIRANDA RICHARDSON
MIKE, *Beth's brother*	PAUL JESSON
LORRAINE, *Jake's mother*	GERALDINE McEWAN
SALLY, *Jake's sister*	RUDI DAVIES
BAYLOR, *Beth's father*	TONY HAYGARTH
MEG, *Beth's mother*	DEBORAH NORTON
THE BAND	BILLY GERAGHTY
	LIAM GRUNDY
	CAROL SLOMAN

Director	Simon Curtis
Designer	Paul Brown
Music	Stephen Warbeck
Lighting Designer	Christopher Toulmin
Sound Designer	Christopher Shutt
Casting Director	Serena Hill
Stage Manager	Karen Little
Deputy Stage Manager	Fiona Bardsley
Assistant Stage Manager	Liz Ainley
Assistant Director	Tim Supple
Production Photographs	John Haynes
Poster design	Iain Lanyon
Photograph	Gerd Kittel

from *Southwest USA*
published by Thames and Hudson

There will be two intervals of fifteen minutes

THE DOGGIE MAN

At a party in playwright Bernard Pomerance's house I fell into conversation with an American guy who owned a greyhound. Though not a doggie man myself I was brought up in Belfast, a whippet's sprint from Dunmore Park where they raced dogs three nights a week, when they weren't racing them at Celtic park, and I had some understanding of the fascination these exotic beasts exerted on gamblers and owners alike. Whether this guy would ever get his dog into a trap at White City I wasn't sure, but he sure as hell looked as if he meant business about something.

What that something was I discovered a few weeks later when the doggie man called by my flat with a play he'd written called Geography of a Horse Dreamer. (O.K. I knew he wrote plays by now, but I still thought of him as the doggie man).

A cowboy, Cody dreams the winners of horse races, is kidnapped by gamblers, loses his gift till he shifts to greyhounds, then he freaks and *becomes* a greyhound before being rescued by his gunslinger brothers. Great writing, wonderful language and like all his plays designed for actors to act in and make their own. So with Bob Hoskins as Beaujo and Ken Cranham as Santee and me as Cody and the doggie man directing we started rehearsals one Monday morning. I've never worked at such speed and with such simplicity. Obstacles were removed rather than erected. Though a raging artist the doggie man was also an austere professional. If we'd known the lines we could have performed the first act by lunchtime Tuesday.

Rehearsals were not orthodox. We had a lot of spare time to play poker and Sam brought in records to illustrate our characters. I sang him an Irish song about a greyhound Master McGrath which he insisted on including in the show.

The London critics weren't impressed by any of it.

We mooched around town together Sam and me, I'm no gambler but I went to the dogs with him, and he would join me in bars, though he didn't drink "because of the Indian blood" he grinned ruefully.

He wrote a beautiful play, called Little Ocean, for three great women, Dinah Stabb, Caroline Hutchinson and O-Lan Shepard and because it was written only for them he vowed no-one else would ever perform it. He asked me to direct it not because I was a director but because a kind of shorthand existed amongst those who knew him and his plays. Nancy Meckler knows his work well and I've since worked with her in several of his plays.

Sam did a lot of work in a short time whilst in London and it was a very rich time for those of us who were involved in it.

Then one day he flew the coop. Back to America, to the West this time avoiding the madness of New York.

It made sense.

The central image in Geography of a Horse Dreamer was quite clear. The artist/dreamer trapped in the anonymous room, the images of his homeland fading, was Sam in London. He is utterly American, the thin air of London was stifling him.

"I've got American scars on my brain" he said. Well he left a few American scars on my Irish cranium and they don't hurt a bit.

STEPHEN REA, 1987

Stephen Rea recently starred in LOST BELONGINGS on Channel 4 and HIGH SOCIETY at Victoria Palace Theatre. He has appeared in a total of four plays by Sam Shepard. BURIED CHILD and KILLER'S HEAD Hampstead Theatre Club directed by Nancy Meckler; ACTION, also directed by Nancy Meckler and GEOGRAPHY OF A HORSE DREAMER (Royal Court Theatre Upstairs). GEOGRAPHY OF A HORSE DREAMER was directed by Sam Shepard.

BIOGRAPHIES

PAUL BROWN — trained under Margaret Harris at Riverside Studios 1984. Recent work includes: FALSTAFF for Graham Vic in the Midlands. At the Royal Court: for Simon Curtis The Young Writers' Festival 1985; OURSELVES ALONE; and ROAD.

SIMON CURTIS— trained as Max Stafford-Clark's Assistant, before directing DEADLINES (Joint Stock/Theatre Upstairs), 1985 Young Writers' Festival, Anne Devlin's OURSELVES ALONE (Liverpool Playhouse/T.U./Main Stage/Irish Tour), Jim Cartright's ROAD (T.U./Main Stage/National Tour) and ROYAL BOROUGH (T.U.). Nominated 1986 Olivier Awards Most Promising Newcomer and is the Royal Court Deputy Director.

RUDI DAVIES — Recent theatre: PENNY FOR A SONG (RSC); TV includes: LIZZIE'S PICTURES, INAPPROPRIATE BEHAVIOUR (BBC); films include: FOREVER YOUNG and THE LONELY PASSION OF JUDITH HEARNE.

BILLY GERAGHTY — began working as actor musician in Community plays in Dorset. Acting includes: Nottingham Playhouse; The Crucible Sheffield; Liverpool Everyman; York Theatre Royal and, more recently, a one-man show for Theatre Foundry and REBEL at the Albany Empire. TV and film include: CONNIE; AUFWIEDERSEN PET; MAGIC HOUR; THE RITZ; CLOSING RANKS. As a musician he has been a drummer, guitarist and vocalist in a number of bands.

LIAM GRUNDY — Music for theatre includes Red Shift; Theatre Venture. Liam has recently produced a single with John Otway following their work on VERBAL DIARY (Edinburgh Festival and UK Tour).

TONY HAYGARTH — Theatre includes: Traverse Theatre Workshop; Open Space Theatre; 7:84 Company; Cambridge Theatre Company; seasons with the RSC and National. TV includes LOVE'S LABOURS LOST; TWO GENTLEMEN OF VERONA; THE INSURANCE MAN; I CLAUDIUS; ROSIE; FARRINGTON OF THE F.O.. Film includes: McVICAR; DRACULA (1979); A PRIVATE FUNCTION; CLOCKWISE; HOLOCAUST; DREAMCHILD.

PAUL JESSON — Theatre includes: BINGO; MARIE AND BRUCE; THE HOUSE; GOOSE PIMPLES; FALKLANDS SOUND/VOCES DE MALVINAS; RENTS; HEDDA GABLER; DEADLINES; THE NORMAL HEART; (Best Supporting Actor, 1986 Olivier Award); THREE SISTERS. Recent TV: WIDOWS; LOVE'S LABOURS LOST; A VERY PECULIAR PRACTICE; INTIMATE CONTACT; QUARTERMAINE'S TERMS; THE RIVALS; FINAL RUN. Film includes: THE PLOUGHMAN'S LUNCH, ACCEPTABLE LEVELS; INTERFERENCE.

GERALDINE McEWAN — Recent theatre: THE BROWNING VERSION; HARLEQUINADE; THE PROVOK'D WIFE; YOU CAN'T TAKE IT WITH YOU; THE RIVALS (National — received the Standard Drama Award as Best Actress) Recent TV includes: Mrs Proudie in THE BARCHESTER CHRONICLES and Lucia in MAPP AND LUCIA.

PAUL MCGANN — For the Royal Court: OI FOR ENGLAND; THE GENIUS. TV includes: GASKIN; MONOCLED MUTINEER; CARIANI AND THE COURTESANS. Film: WITHNAIL AND I (released in 1988).

DEBORAH NORTON — Most recently at the Royal Court: INADMISSIBLE EVIDENCE and THE LONDON CUCKOLDS; and elsewhere: A LITTLE HOTEL ON THE SIDE (National Theatre); CALIFORNIA DOG FIGHT (Bush); BARNABY AND THE OLD BOYS (Theatr Clwyd). TV includes: THE PEDLER; INSTANT ENLIGHTENMENT INCLUDING VAT; THE EXECUTIONER; HINKLEY HOUSE; HITTING TOWN; ROUND AND ROUND; ARENA (Presenter); and currently YES, PRIME MINISTER. Films: LIVING TOGETHER; HOLOCAUST; WILD CATS OF ST TRINIANS; MUSSOLINI COUNTRY; VIOLENT SUMMER. Deborah has reviewed books and radio for The Sunday Times.

WILL PATTON — New York: Extensive work with Joseph Chaikin and The Winter Project; Lew Jenkin's DARK RIDE and LIMBO TALES (Villager Award); David Rabe's GOOSE AND TOM TOM (Villager Award); Sam Shepard's own production of A LIE OF THE MIND (playing Mike). Recent TV: A GATHERING OF OLD MEN. Films include: SILKWOOD; AFTER HOURS; DESPERATELY SEEKING SUSAN; NO WAY OUT and soon to be released, STARS AND BARS with Daniel Day Lewis.

MIRANDA RICHARDSON — For the Royal Court: EDMOND. Theatre includes: INSIGNIFICANCE, and WHO'S AFRAID OF VIRGINIA WOOLF (Bristol). TV includes: BLACK ADDER; DEATH OF THE HEART; AFTER PILKINGTON. Film includes: DANCE WITH A STRANGER; THE INNOCENT; EMPIRE OF THE SUN (to be released).

CAROL SLOMAN — read music at London University and trained as a classical pianist. Music work includes: Chichester Festival; Sheffield Crucible; Duke's Playhouse Lancaster; Manchester Contact. Acting includes: LENNON (Olivier Award Nomination); THE MOTHER. Composed music and lyrics for CRAZY by Stephen Bill and SHADOW OF A DOUBT (Avon Touring Company).

CHRISTOPHER TOULMIN — has been at the Royal Court for 6½ years, during which time he has lit several productions including: PANIC; OURSELVES ALONE; THE GRACE OF MARY TRAVERSE; AUNT DAN AND LEMON; and ROAD. Work outside the Court has included: Liverpool Playhouse (Studio); GAUDETE at The Almeida; THE SEAGULL at the Sherman Cardiff; and most recently SANCTUARY for Joint Stock.

STEPHEN WARBECK — has composed music for: THE CAUCASIAN CHALK CIRCLE (Thames TV and Oxford Playhouse); THE GOOD PERSON OF SETZUAN; THE MOTHER (National Theatre); COMEDY OF ERRORS. For the Royal Court: BUILT ON SAND, ROYAL BOROUGH. Other theatre includes: Glasgow Citizens; Manchester Royal Exchange, The Young Vic; Oxford Playhouse; Liverpool Playhouse; Liverpool Everyman; Theatre Royal Stratford East.

FOR THE ROYAL COURT THEATRE

DIRECTION:
Artistic Director..............MAX STAFFORD-CLARK
Deputy Director..............,..........SIMON CURTIS
Assistant Directors..............LINDSAY POSNER, TIM SUPPLE
Casting Director..............LISA MAKIN
Literary Manager..............KATE HARWOOD
Senior Script Associate..............MICHAEL HASTINGS*
Secretary..............MELANIE KENYON

PRODUCTION:
Production Manager..............BO BARTON
Technical Manager, Theatre Upstairs..............CHRIS BAGUST
Chief Electrician..............CHRISTOPHER TOULMIN
Deputy Chief Electricians..............ACE McCARRON , MARK BRADLEY
Sound Designer..............CHRISTOPHER SHUTT
Master Carpenter..............CHRIS HARDING-ROBERTS
Deputy Carpenter..............JOHN BURGESS
Costume Supervisor..............JENNIFER COOK
Wardrobe Assistant..............CATHIE SKILBECK

ADMINISTRATION:
General Manager..............GRAHAM COWLEY
Secretary..............ROSALEEN DEW
Financial Administrator..............EILEEN WENTWORTH
Press & Publicity Manager..............SHARON KEAN
Press & Publicity, Theatre Upstairs..............NATASHA HARVEY
House Manager..............GILL RUSSELL
Assistant House Manager..............ALISON SMITH
Membership Secretary..............SUSIE BREAKELL*
Box Office Manager..............CHRISTOPHER PEARCY
Box Office Assistants..............PAT GIBBONS, SALLY HARRIS, DEBBIE SMITH
Stage Door/Telephonist..............DIANE PETHERICK*, ANGELA TOULMIN*
Evening Stage Door..............TYRONE LUCAS*, CERI SHIELDS*
Maintenance..............JOHN LORRIGIO*
Cleaners..............EILEEN CHAPMAN*, IVY JONES*, CLIFF WOOTTON*
Firemen..............MICK BROWN*, PAUL KLEINMANN*

YOUNG PEOPLE'S THEATRE
Director..............ELYSE DODGSON
Administrator..............JANE HELLINGS
Youth Drama Worker..............SUZY GILMOUR
Schools & Community Liaison Worker..............MARK HOLNESS
Writer in Residence..............KARIM ALRAWI

*Part-time staff

COUNCIL: Chairman: MATTHEW EVANS. CHRIS BAGUST, BO BARTON, STUART BURGE, ANTHONY C BURTON, CARYL CHURCHILL, HARRIET CRUICKSHANK, SIMON CURTIS, ALLAN DAVIS, DAVID LLOYD DAVIS, ROBERT FOX, MRS HENNY GESTETNER OBE, DEREK GRANGER, DAVID HARE, JOCELYN HERBERT, DAVID KLEEMAN, HANIF KUREISHI, SONIA MELCHETT, JOAN PLOWRIGHT CBE, GREVILLE POKE, JANE RAYNE, SIR HUGH WILLATT.

A Lie of the Mind was first performed at the Promenade Theater in New York on December 5, 1985. It was produced by Lewis Allen and Stephen Graham. The director was Sam Shepard.

The cast was as follows:

JAKE	Harvey Keitel
FRANKIE	Aidan Quinn
BETH	Amanda Plummer
MIKE	Will Patton
LORRAINE	Geraldine Page
SALLY	Karen Young
BAYLOR	James Gammon
MEG	Ann Wedgeworth

Dedicated to the memory of L.P.

Something identifies you with the one who leaves you, and it is your common power to return: thus your greatest sorrow.

Something separates you from the one who remains with you, and it is your common slavery to depart: thus your meagerest rejoicing.

—Cesar Vallejo

· · ·

Most were bankrupt small farmers or down-at-the-heel city proletarians, and the rest were mainly chronic nomads of the sort who, a century later, roved the country in caricatures of automobiles. If they started for Kentucky or Ohio, they were presently moving on to Indiana or Illinois, and after that, doggedly and irrationally, to even wilder and less hospitable regions. When they halted, it was simply because they had become exhausted.

—H. L. Mencken, *The American Language*

SET DESCRIPTION

Proscenium oriented but with space played out in front of arch. Deep, wide, dark space with a four-foot-wide ramp extreme upstage, suspended about twelve feet high, stretching from stage right to stage left. When unlit, the ramp should disappear. Extreme downstage right (from actor's p.o.v.) is a platform, set about a foot off the floor, wide enough to accommodate the actors and furniture. The platform continues upstage to about the middle of the stage, then abruptly stops. Center stage is wide open, bare, and left at floor level. The impression should be of infinite space, going off to nowhere. Extreme stage left is another platform, slightly larger than the stage right one and elevated about three feet off floor level. This entire construction of ramp, platforms, and stage floor is fixed and dark in color. In the first act there are no walls to define locations—only furniture and props and light in the bare space. In the second and third acts walls are brought in to delineate the rooms on either side of the stage. Only two walls on each platform, with no ceilings. In the case of the stage-right platform, a wall with a window, extreme stage right. Another wall tying into it, upstage right, running perpendicular to it and with a door in the stage-left side of it. The downstage and stage-left sides of the platform are left open. On the stage-left platform, two more walls set the same way but leaving the downstage and stage-right sides of the platform wide open. An old-style swinging kitchen door is set in the stage-right side of the upstage wall. A window in the stage-left wall.

MUSIC NOTES

In the original New York production, which I directed, I had the good fortune to encounter a bluegrass group called the Red Clay Ramblers, out of Chapel Hill, North Carolina. Their musical sensibilities, musicianship, and great repertoire of traditional and original tunes fit the play like a glove. It would be stretching the limitations of this publication to include all the lyrics and music notations that were such an integral part of that production. But working intimately with these musicians, structuring bridges between scenes, underscoring certain monologues, and developing musical "themes" to open and close the acts left me no doubt that this play needs music. Live music. Music with an American backbone.

Since every director must develop his own personal sense of the material he's working on, I will leave the choice of music up to him. All I ask is that there *be* music and that the music serve to support the emotional values discovered by the actors in the course of rehearsal.

I would also like to thank the Red Clay Ramblers for their tremendous contribution to our original production of this play.

—SAM SHEPARD

Act I

SCENE 1

FRANKIE, *behind audience holding a telephone, talking into it, walking in tight circles, kicking the cord out of his way.* JAKE, *upstage left on suspended platform, suitcase beside him, standing at a blue payphone on highway, talking into it. Pale yellow full moon extreme upstage right center. Impression of huge dark space and distance between the two characters with each one isolated in his own pool of light. Their voices are heard, first in pitch black. The moon comes up very softly as their conversation continues in the dark, then light slowly begins to reveal the two characters.*

FRANKIE: *(In dark)* Jake. Jake? Now, look—Jake? Listen. Just listen to me a second.

(Sound of JAKE smashing receiver down on payphone.)

Jake! Don't do that! You're gonna disconnect us again. Listen to me. Gimme the number where you are, okay? Just gimme the number.

JAKE: *(In dark)* There's no number!

FRANKIE: There must be a number.

JAKE: I can't read it!

FRANKIE: Just gimme the number so I can call you back if we get disconnected again.

JAKE: There's no number! It's dark! I can't read in the dark! Whad'ya think I am, an owl or somethin'!

1

FRANKIE: Okay, okay. Take it easy. Where are you then?

JAKE: Highway 2.

FRANKIE: What state?

JAKE: Some state. I don't know. They're all the same up here.

FRANKIE: Try to think.

JAKE: I don't need to think! I know! *(Pause)* You shoulda seen her face, Frankie. You shoulda seen it.

FRANKIE: Beth?

JAKE: I never even seen it comin'. I shoulda known. Why didn't I see it comin'. I been good for so long.

FRANKIE: Just try not to think about it for right now, Jake. Okay? Just try to let go of the thought of it.

JAKE: It's not a thought. Don't gimme that Zen shit.

FRANKIE: The picture then. Whatever—

JAKE: It's not a picture either! It's her. I see her. She's right here with me now!

FRANKIE: She's there?

JAKE: She's here! She's right here!

FRANKIE: Beth's there with you?

(JAKE *smashes down on receiver again. Pools of light up now on* BOTH *of them. Moon full.)*

Jake! Stop doing that, will ya! Just take it easy. Jake? You still there? (Pause) Jake! Don't hang up on me.

(Pause)

JAKE: She's not gonna pull outa this one, Frankie. She's not gonna. I saw her face. It was bad this time. Real bad.

FRANKIE: What happened?

JAKE: All red and black and blue.

FRANKIE: Oh, Jake—God. What'd you do?

JAKE: I never even saw it comin', Frankie. I never did. How come that is? How come?

FRANKIE: Where is she now?

JAKE: She's dead!

(Pause)

FRANKIE: What?

JAKE: She's dead!

(JAKE *puts receiver down softly and hangs up this time.*)

FRANKIE: Jake! Jake! Goddamnit!

(FRANKIE *slams his receiver down. Blackout. Moon stays full.*)

SCENE 2

BETH's *voice is heard in blackout almost overlapping* FRANKIE's *last line. Lights up fast on* BETH *downstage left as she sits up straight with a jerk as though awakened by a nightmare. She is in a white hospital bed covered with a sheet. She wears a blue hospital smock. Her head is wrapped in bandages. Her face badly bruised, eyes black and blue. Her brother,* MIKE, *stands behind her upstage of bed, arm around her shoulder, stroking her back. She tries to speak but no words come, just short punctuated sounds at the end of her rapid exhales.*

BETH: Saah—thah—Jaah—thuh—saah—saah—saah—saah—

(Continues under.)

MIKE: *(Stroking her back)* Don't talk, Beth. You don't have to talk. It's all right, honey.

*(*BETH *discovers bandage on her head and starts to rip it off. It starts to come apart in long streamers of gauze.* MIKE *tries to stop her but she continues tearing the bandage off.)*

BETH: *(As she rips off bandage)* Ghaah—ghaah—khaah— khaah—khaah—

(Continues)

MIKE: No, leave that on. Leave it, Beth. You're supposed to leave it on for a while. Don't take that off.

BETH: *(Still pulling bandage off)* Am I a mummy now? Am I a mummy? Am I? Am I now?

4

MIKE: It's just a bandage.

BETH: *(Rapid speech; it gushes out of her)* You tell them, I'm not dead. You go tell them. Tell them now. Go tell them. Dig me up. Tell them dig me up now. I'm not in here. They can't wait for me now.

MIKE: Beth, it's all right.

BETH: Are they above us now? How deep are we in here? How deep?

MIKE: It's okay.

BETH: They leave you here to bring me back? Did they leave you?

MIKE: It's a hospital, Beth.

BETH: Iza toomb! Iza toomb! You tell them I'm not dead! Go tell them!

MIKE: Beth, it's okay. You got hurt but you're gonna be all right now.

BETH: Did they bury me in a tree? A tribe? Did they?

(MIKE holds her firmly by the shoulders. Pause. BETH feels her head.)

Whaaza plase where I fell? Who fell me?

MIKE: *(Holding her)* You're okay.

(Both BETH's arms shoot straight up above her head. She holds them there stiffly.)

BETH: *(Screams, holds her arms up)* WHO FELL ME!!!

MIKE: *(Trying to bring her arms down to her sides)* Beth. I'm with you now. I'll take care of you. Do you recognize me? You know who I am?

(BETH stares at him, slowly relaxes her arms, brings them back down to her sides. MIKE strokes her back softly.)

BETH: Yore the dog. Yore the dog they send.

MIKE: I'm Mike. I'm your brother.

BETH: Mike the dog.

(She spits in his face. Pause.)

MIKE: I'm gonna stay with you now.

BETH: You gant take in me. You gant take me back.

MIKE: I'm not going to take you anywhere. We'll stay right here until you're all better.

BETH: Who fell me here?

MIKE: Don't worry about that.

BETH: Who fell me? Iza—Iza name? Iza name to come. Itz— Itz— Inza man. Inza—name. Aall—aall—all—a love. A love.

MIKE: Don't try to talk, Beth. You just need some rest now.

BETH: *(Soft)* Heez with you?

MIKE: No.

BETH: Heez—

MIKE: He's gone now. He's not around. Don't worry about him. He's nowhere near here.

BETH: Don' leeve me.

MIKE: I won't, honey. I promise. I'll stay right here with you.

(Pause)

BETH: *(Soft, weeping)* Whaaz he gone?

MIKE: He's far away. He won't hurt you now.

BETH: Heez—

MIKE: Just try to get some sleep now, honey. Try to get some sleep.

BETH: Heez gone.

(Lights fade. Moon stays full but turns pale green.)

SCENE 3

Soft orange light up on stage-right platform, revealing small ragged motel couch with a floor lamp beside it. Main light source emanating from lamp. A wooden chair opposite couch. JAKE's *suitcase on floor with clothes spilled out of it.* JAKE *sits in middle of couch, legs apart, slouched forward, holding his head in his hands.* FRANKIE *stands behind couch with a plastic bag full of ice, trying to apply it to the back of* JAKE's *neck.* JAKE *keeps pushing the ice away.*

JAKE: *(Shoving ice away)* I don't want any goddamn ice! It's cold!

FRANKIE: I thought it might help.

JAKE: Well, it don't. It's cold.

FRANKIE: I know it's cold. It's ice. It's supposed to be cold.

(Pause)

*(*FRANKIE *goes to chair. Sits. Silence between them for a while.)*

You didn't actually kill her, did ya, Jake?

*(*JAKE *stays seated. Starts slow, low, deliberate.)*

JAKE: She was goin' to these goddamn rehearsals every day. Every day. Every single day. Hardly ever see her. I saw enough though. Believe you me. Saw enough to know somethin' was goin' on.

FRANKIE: But you didn't really kill her, did ya?

7

JAKE: *(Builds)* I'm no dummy. Doesn't take much to put it together. Woman starts dressin' more and more skimpy every time she goes out. Starts puttin' on more and more smells. Oils. She was always oiling herself before she went out. Every morning. Smell would wake me up. Coconut or Butterscotch or some goddamn thing. Sweet stuff. Youda thought she was an ice-cream sundae. I'd watch her oiling herself while I pretended to be asleep. She was in a dream, the way she did it. Like she was imagining someone else touching her. Not me. Never me. Someone else.

FRANKIE: Who?

JAKE: *(Stands, moves around space, gains momentum)* Some guy. I don't know. Some actor-jerk. I knew she was gettin' herself ready for him. I could tell. Got worse and worse. When I finally called her on it she denied it flat. I knew she was lying too. Could tell it right away. The way she took it so light. Tried to cast it off like it was nothin'. Then she starts tellin' me it's all in *my* head. Some imaginary deal I'd cooked up in *my* head. Had nothin' to do with her, she said. Made me try to believe I was crazy. She's all innocent and I'm crazy. So I told her—I told her—I laid it on the line to her. Square business. I says—no more high heels! No more wearin' them high spiky high heels to rehearsals. No more a' that shit. And she laughs. Right to my face. She laughs. Kept puttin' 'em on. Every mornin'. Puttin' 'em back on. She says it's right for the part. Made her feel like the character she says. Then I told her she had to wear a bra and she paid no attention to that either. You could see right through her damn blouse. Right clean through it. And she never wore underpants either. That's what really got me. No underpants. You could see everything.

FRANKIE: Well, she never wore underpants anyway, did she?

*(*JAKE *stops, turns to* FRANKIE. FRANKIE *stays in chair. Pause.)*

JAKE: How do you know?

FRANKIE: No, I mean—I think you told me once.

JAKE: *(Moving slowly toward* FRANKIE*)* I never told you that. I never woulda told you a thing like that. That's personal.

FRANKIE: *(Backing up)* No, I think you did once—when you were drunk or somethin'.

JAKE: *(Close to* FRANKIE*)* I never woulda told you that!

FRANKIE: All right.

(Pause)

JAKE: I never talked about her that way to anybody.

FRANKIE: Okay. Forget it. Just forget it.

JAKE: You always liked her, didn't you, Frankie? Don't think I overlooked that.

FRANKIE: Are you gonna finish tellin' me what happened? 'Cause if you're not I'm gonna take a walk right outa here.

(Pause. JAKE *considers, then launches back into the story.)*

JAKE: *(Returns to speed, moves)* Okay. Then she starts readin' the lines with me, at night. In bed. Readin' the lines. I'm helpin' her out, right? Helpin' her memorize the damn lines so she can run off every morning and say 'em to some other guy. Day after day. Same lines. And these lines are all about how she's bound and determined to get this guy back in the sack with her after all these years he's been ignoring her. How she still loves him even though he hates her. How she's saving her body up for him and him only.

FRANKIE: Well, it was just a play, wasn't it?

JAKE: Yeah, a play. That's right. Just a play. "Pretend." That's what she said. "Just pretend." I know what they were doing! I know damn well what they were doin'! I know what that acting shit is all about. They try to "believe" they're the person. Right? Try to believe so hard they're the person that they actually think they become the person. So you know what that means don't ya?

FRANKIE: What?

JAKE: They start doin' all the same stuff the person does!

FRANKIE: What person?

JAKE: The person! The—whad'ya call it? The—

FRANKIE: Character?

JAKE: Yeah. The character. That's right. They start acting that way in real life. Just like the character. Walkin' around—talkin' that way. You shoulda seen the way she started to walk and talk. I couldn't believe it. Changed her hair and everything. Put a wig on. Changed her clothes. Everything changed. She was unrecognizable. I didn't even know who I was with anymore. I told her. I told her, look—"I don't know who you think you are now but I'd just as soon you come on back to the real world here." And you know what she tells me?

FRANKIE: What?

JAKE: She tells me this is the real world. This acting shit is more real than the real world to her. Can you believe that? And she was tryin' to convince me that *I* was crazy?

(Pause)

FRANKIE: So you think she was sleeping with this guy just because she was playing a part in a play?

JAKE: Yeah. She was real dedicated.

FRANKIE: Are you sure? I mean when would she have time to do that in rehearsals?

JAKE: On her lunch break.

FRANKIE: *(Stands)* Oh, come on, Jake.

JAKE: Sit down! Sit back down. I got more to tell you.

FRANKIE: No! I'm not gonna sit down! I came to try to help you out and all you're tellin' me is a bunch of bullshit about Beth screwing around with some other guy on her lunch break?

JAKE: She was! It's easy to tell when a woman gets obsessed with somethin' else. When she moves away from you. They don't hide it as easy as men.

FRANKIE: She was just trying to do a good job.

JAKE: That's no job! I've had jobs before. I know what a job is. A job is where you work. A job is where you don't have fun. You don't dick around tryin' to pretend you're somebody else. You work. Work is work!

FRANKIE: It's a different kind of a job.

JAKE: It's an excuse to fool around! That's what it is. That's why she wanted to become an actress in the first place. So she could get away from me.

FRANKIE: You can't jump to that kind of conclusion just because she was—

JAKE: I didn't jump to nothin'! I knew what she was up to even if she didn't.

FRANKIE: So, you mean you're accusing her of somethin' she wasn't even aware of?

JAKE: She was aware all right. She was tryin' to hide it from me but she wasn't that good an actress.

(Pause)

FRANKIE: So you beat her up again. Boy, I'm tellin' you—

JAKE: I killed her.

(Pause)

FRANKIE: You killed her.

JAKE: That's right.

FRANKIE: She stopped breathing?

JAKE: Everything stopped.

FRANKIE: You checked?

JAKE: I didn't have to check.

FRANKIE: She might've just been unconscious or something.

JAKE: No.

FRANKIE: Well, what'd you do? Did you tell the police?

JAKE: Why would I do that? She was already dead. What could they
do about it?

FRANKIE: That's what you're supposed to do when somebody dies.
You report it to the police.

JAKE: Even when you kill 'em?

FRANKIE: Yeah! Even when you kill them. Especially when you kill
them!

JAKE: I never heard a' that.

(Pause)

FRANKIE: Well, somebody should check up on it. I mean this is pretty
serious stuff, Jake.

JAKE: I done my time for her. I already done my time.

FRANKIE: She had nothin' to do with that. She never did.

JAKE: She got me in trouble more'n once. She did it on purpose too.
Always flirtin' around. Always carryin' on.

FRANKIE: She had nothin' to do with it! You lost your temper.

JAKE: She provoked it!

FRANKIE: You've always lost your temper and blamed it on somebody else. Even when you were a kid you blamed it on somebody
else. One time you even blamed it on a goat. I remember
that.

(Pause. JAKE stops.)

JAKE: What goat?

FRANKIE: That milk goat we had.

JAKE: What was her name?

FRANKIE: I forget.

JAKE: What was that goat's name?

FRANKIE: You remember that goat?

JAKE: Yeah, I remember that goat. I loved that goat.

FRANKIE: Well you kicked the shit out of that goat you loved so much when she stepped on your bare feet while you were tryin' to milk her. You remember that? Broke her ribs.

JAKE: I never kicked that goat!

FRANKIE: Oh, you don't remember that huh? You broke your damn foot you kicked her so hard.

JAKE: What was that goat's name?

(JAKE suddenly falls to the floor, collapses. FRANKIE goes to him. Tries to help him.)

Get away from me!

FRANKIE: What happened?

JAKE: Just get away!

FRANKIE: You all right?

JAKE: Somethin's wrong. My head's funny.

FRANKIE: *(Trying to help JAKE up)* Come on, let's get you back on the couch.

JAKE: *(Pushing FRANKIE away, crawls on knees toward couch)* I don't need any help!

FRANKIE: You feel dizzy or something?

JAKE: *(Crawling to couch)* Yeah. All of a sudden. Everything's—

FRANKIE: You want me to get you something?

JAKE: *(Climbing up on couch and lying on his belly)* No. I don't need nothin'.

FRANKIE: You want me to get a doctor for you?

JAKE: I'm gonna die without her. I know I'm gonna die.

(Pause)

FRANKIE: I could go to her folks' place. They'd know what happened to her.

JAKE: No! You stay away from there! Don't go anywhere near there. I'm through chasin' after her.

FRANKIE: Somebody's gotta find out, Jake. Sooner or later.

(Pause. JAKE speaks in a whisper, almost to himself. His whole tone changes. Very vulnerable, as though questioning a ghost.)

JAKE: Now. Why now? Why am I missing her now, Frankie? Why not then? When she was there? Why am I afraid I'm gonna lose her when she's already gone? And this fear—this fear swarms through me—floods my whole body till there's nothing left. Nothing left of me. And then it turns— It turns to a fear for my whole life. Like my whole life is lost from losing her. Gone. That I'll die like this. Lost. Just lost.

FRANKIE: It's okay, Jake.

JAKE: You liked her too, didn't you, Frankie?

FRANKIE: Yeah. I liked her.

(Pause)

JAKE: My back's like ice. How come my back's so cold?

FRANKIE: *(Moves right)* I'll get you a blanket.

JAKE: No! Don't leave.

FRANKIE: *(Stops)* All right.

(Pause)

You okay?

JAKE: Yeah. Just sit with me for a while. Stay here.

FRANKIE: *(Goes to chair, pulls it near couch)* Okay.

(FRANKIE sits in chair next to couch. JAKE stays on his belly, arm hanging limply over the side of couch, hand touching the floor.)

JAKE: Don't leave.

FRANKIE: I won't.

(Lights dim to black.)

SCENE 4

Lights up extreme left on MIKE *trying to help* BETH *walk. Her arm is around his neck. His arm around her waist and the other hand holding her hand. Her legs are very weak and keep going out from under her periodically. Sometimes he reaches down and moves one of her legs forward when she appears too weak to move. She stops now and then, breathing hard from the effort. She watches her bare feet the whole time, then once in a while her head jerks up and stares at the ceiling, then back down to her feet again—similar to the head movements of a blind person. The two of them keep struggling to walk in circles like this as they speak.* BETH's *voice now is very childlike and small.*

BETH: *(As she walks)* You won' hurd him, Mige. Yera kineness. Alla kineness. In for nah to me. Fine I kim it.

MIKE: *(Helping her walk)* Just try to keep moving. That's it. You're doing great.

BETH: Yera kineness, Mige. I'm onah too. Fo fo nahchoo. Inah laan tobit. In a laan.

MIKE: Try to pay attention to walking, honey. Just walking. You don't have to talk now. Doctor said that would come later. Slow. You don't have to worry about that now.

BETH: Jess walk. No makin' fan tat. Sant. Sant. *(She giggles.)*

MIKE: That's right.

BETH: Jess step. Ah kahn tah.

16

MIKE: Take it slow.

BETH: You won' hurd them. You won'. Nah can't a chile. A chile. Ah chile. *(Like "child")* You can hurd him, Mige. Hee a chile. Both.

MIKE: Don't think about him now. We'll worry about him later. Right now you just have to get strong. You have to learn how to walk first.

BETH: Heez nah weak. He bash me. *(She giggles.)* Bash me goot.

MIKE: *(Hard)* DON'T THINK ABOUT HIM!

(BETH stops, clasps her arms across her chest and folds completely forward. Her head drops. She starts to weep.)

(MIKE hugs her, trying to straighten her up.)

Beth, I'm sorry. I'm sorry. I—I just want you to concentrate so you can get better. That's all. Okay? I'm sorry. I want you to walk so we can take you home. You understand? Mom and Dad want to see you. Don't you want to get better?

(BETH shakes her head defiantly, stays folded up.)

Don't you want to get back home?

(Suddenly BETH pulls away from MIKE, takes a few steps on her own and falls. MIKE goes to her fast and picks her back up on her feet.)

BETH: *(Savage)* NO! DON' TUSH ME!

MIKE: *(Holding her up as she struggles)* I have to hold you up, Beth, or you'll fall over.

BETH: DON' TUSH ME! I won' fall! I won'.

MIKE: All right. If you want to stand on your own, that's great.

BETH: I won'.

MIKE: Okay.

(MIKE cautiously lets go of her and stands back a couple steps, ready to catch her if she topples. BETH just stands there for a while staring at her feet. She sways slightly from side to side.)

BETH: *(Quietly, staring at her feet)* I'm above my feet. Way above. Inah—I cah—

MIKE: Can you take a step?

BETH: How high me? How high—up?

MIKE: Try to take a step, Beth.

BETH: How high? Did they bury me in a tree?

MIKE: Try taking a step.

BETH: *(Abrupt, jerks her head toward MIKE)* You! You ztep.

(Pause)

MIKE: You want me to take a step?

BETH: *(Staying in the same place)* You ztep.

MIKE: If I take a step, will you take one?

BETH: You!

MIKE: All right.

(MIKE takes a step. BETH laughs. Stays in place.)

What's so funny?

BETH: You ztep. Fan tak. You.

MIKE: You want to try?

BETH: No! You.

MIKE: I just took one. Now it's your turn.

BETH: *(Clearly, rage)* I'M NOT A BABY! I'M NOT!

(Pause)

MIKE: I know you're not, Beth. I just want you to try to take a step. That's all.

BETH: NO!

(Pause as BETH *stands there, rooted to the spot, but still swaying slightly.)*

MIKE: Well, what're you gonna do, just stand there?

BETH: *(Fast, very clear, mimicking him exactly)* Well, what're you gonna do, just stand there?

MIKE: *(Moving closer to her)* Beth.

BETH: *(Screams)* DON' TUSH ME!

*(*MIKE *stops. Stands off from her.* BETH *stays still, swaying, staring down at her feet. Pause.)*

MIKE: I'm just trying to help you out.

(Pause. BETH's *head jerks up. She stares at ceiling and stays.)*

BETH: Hee killed us both.

MIKE: *(Moves toward her, then stops)* You're not dead, Beth. You're going to be all right.

BETH: *(Fierce, jerks her head toward* MIKE*)* I'M DEAD! DEAD! DAAAAH! HEEZ TOO.

MIKE: You gotta forget about him for now! You gotta just forget about him!

BETH: NAAH! You gan' stop my head. Nobody! Nobody stop my head. My head is me. Heez in me. You gan stop him in me. Nobody gan stop him in me.

MIKE: This guy tried to kill you! How can you still want a man who tried to kill you! What's the matter with you! He's the one who did this to you!

BETH: HEEZ MY HAAAAAAAAAAAAAAAART!!!

(Blackout. Moon stays green and full.)

SCENE 5

Lights up fast down right. Same props as Scene 3. Couch and lamp, suitcase, clothes, etc. But now more of the area is lit in front and to the sides of the couch with the couch remaining in very dim light. Just able to make out the shape of JAKE *lying belly down still, with his face turned away from audience, covered with blanket, arm still dangling out over the side.* FRANKIE, *his sister,* SALLY, *and their mother,* LORRAINE, *enter fast from upstage right of platform and cross down center into middle neutral territory. Scene is played out down center for a while.*

FRANKIE:*(On the move, entering from up right)* Just try to keep your voice down, Mom. This is the first time he's slept since I've seen him.

LORRAINE: Don't be so damn bossy.

FRANKIE: Well, he hasn't slept.

LORRAINE: I just wanna take a look at him is all.

SALLY: Mom—

FRANKIE: He's not lookin' too good right now, Mom.

LORRAINE: What'sa matter with him?

FRANKIE: He's lost a whole bunch of weight.

LORRAINE: Well, I'll make him up a batch a' that cream of broccoli soup. That'll put the weight back on him. That's his favorite.

FRANKIE: He won't eat.

21

LORRAINE: Whad'ya mean he won't eat. That boy'll eat the paint off a plate if you let him. Whad'ya been feedin' him?

FRANKIE: He's in big trouble, Mom.

LORRAINE: So what's new? Name a day he wasn't in trouble. He was trouble from day one. Fell on his damn head the second he was born. Slipped right through the doctor's fingers. That's where it all started. Back there. Had nothin' to do with his upbringing.

SALLY: Mom, just listen to Frankie a second. He's tryin' to tell you somethin'.

LORRAINE: I am listenin' but I'm not hearin' no revelations! What's the story here? My boy's sick. I'll make him some soup. We'll take him out to the Drive-In. Everything's gonna be fine. What's the big deal here?

SALLY: Mom! Jake might've killed Beth! That's what's goin' on. All right?

(Pause)

LORRAINE: Who's Beth?

(Pause)

SALLY: Oh, my God. Jake's wife. Beth. You remember her? Beth? Little, skinny Beth?

LORRAINE: Never heard a' her.

SALLY: Mom—Mom, you don't remember Beth?

LORRAINE: No. Why should I? I don't keep track of his bimbos.

SALLY: Great.

FRANKIE: We're not really sure about it yet, Mom. I mean—he's pretty emotional about the whole thing.

LORRAINE: He's an emotional boy. Always has been.

SALLY: He's not a boy. He's a big grown-up man and he might have killed his wife!

LORRAINE: He wasn't fit to live with anybody to begin with! I don't know why he ever tried it. Woman who lives with a man like that deserves to be killed. She deserves it.

FRANKIE: All right, knock it off! Both a' you! We gotta think about this thing now. Jake's the one who's in trouble here, okay? He's in bad shape. You understand that? He's in real bad shape. Every day he's gettin' worse.

SALLY: He's not gonna die or anything—

LORRAINE: My boy ain't gonna die. I'm goin' in there right now and nobody's gonna stop me.

(LORRAINE *moves directly onto stage-right platform toward the couch and* JAKE, *pushing past* FRANKIE, *who makes no attempt to stop her. Lights rise on couch now, equal to the rest of area. She stops beside couch and swats* JAKE *hard on the rump.* JAKE *doesn't move.* FRANKIE *and* SALLY *follow her onto platform.)*

Jake? Jake, it's your mother. Sit up, boy. Sit up and lemme take a look at your tongue. Come on, now. Sit up and face me.

(JAKE *rolls over slowly, facing out toward audience now. His face is pale white, eyes sunken and dark, radically changed from the last time he was seen.* LORRAINE *steps back.* FRANKIE *and* SALLY *move into couch area with* LORRAINE.)

(To FRANKIE)

What in the hell's he got? He looks like death warmed over.

SALLY: Jake?

(JAKE *just stares at them.)*

LORRAINE: *(To* JAKE*)* Your brother here's been tryin' to tell us that you're gonna pass on us. Now quit the shenanigans and sit up. Jake? Are you hearin' me?

SALLY: Just leave him be, Mom.

LORRAINE: He's just playacting. Used to do this all the time when he didn't get his own way. Mope around for days like a cocker spaniel. Got so bad sometimes I finally had to take a bucket a' ice cold rainwater and throw it right in his damn face. That worked every time. Maybe that's what we oughta do right now. *(To* FRANKIE*)* You got a bucket?

FRANKIE: I don't think rainwater's gonna do it, Mom. He's had the chills for three days now. He just shakes all through the night. Talks to himself and shakes.

LORRAINE: It's all pretend. He just wants some attention, that's all.

*(*SALLY *moves closer to* JAKE. *He smiles at her.)*

SALLY: Jake? You feelin' any better?

JAKE: *(Soft, loving)* How'd you ever get to be so beautiful?

SALLY: *(Short laugh)* You never used to think that when we were kids. Least you never admitted it. You always called me the Crayfish. You remember?

JAKE: *(Slow, slurred)* We were never gonna be apart.

SALLY: Jake, you know who I am, don't ya?

JAKE: We were gonna be tied together. *(Laughs.)* You remember when I tied you to me. That one night. You tried sneakin' off on me. In my sleep. Couldn't do it, could ya? Couldn't. Had you tied.

LORRAINE: *(Moving to* FRANKIE, *taking him aside so* JAKE *can't hear. To* FRANKIE*)* Has he been drinkin' or somethin'?

FRANKIE: No, I wouldn't buy him a bottle. Are you kidding?

LORRAINE: Well don't. Not unless you want someone else killed.

FRANKIE: I'm not gonna.

LORRAINE: Every time he gets near liquor he thinks it's his God-given duty to keep pace with his old man.

FRANKIE: I know that.

LORRAINE: Don't you dare buy him a bottle.

FRANKIE: I won't!

(JAKE *reaches out suddenly and grabs* SALLY *by the wrist. She pulls back but his grip is powerful.*)

SALLY: Jake, come on!

LORRAINE: *(Moving back to* JAKE, *to* JAKE*)* You let go a' yer sister!

JAKE: *(To* SALLY, *keeping hold of her wrist)* I was sure—I was so damn sure we both had the same idea. I was sure a' that.

SALLY: *(Pulling back slightly but caught)* I'm Sally, Jake. Your sister. Sally. Now let go a' me, all right?

LORRAINE: He knows who you are. Don't you believe for one minute that he don't know who you are. *(Approaching* JAKE.*)* You know who she is, now let go of her! Let go of her right now.

JAKE: You never did see me, did ya, Beth? Just had a big wild notion about some dream life up ahead. Somebody who was gonna save yer ass.

(JAKE *starts to bear down on* SALLY's *wrist now and drags her closer to him.*)

SALLY: *(Scared, struggling to get free)* I'm not Beth, Jake! Let go a' me. Let go a' me! You're hurtin' me!

LORRAINE: Let go a' your sister!

(LORRAINE *takes off one of her shoes, charges* JAKE *and starts belting him over the head with it.* JAKE *keeps hold of* SALLY's *wrist.* FRANKIE *moves in and pulls* LORRAINE *away from* JAKE *from behind. She starts to beat* FRANKIE *with the shoe now.*)

JAKE: *(To* SALLY*)* I'm gonna let go a' you! I'm gonna let go a' you once and for all!

*(*JAKE *drops* SALLY*'s wrist.* SALLY *backs away fast, rubbing her wrist.* JAKE*'s arm falls limply to the floor again. His eyes close. He goes unconscious.* LORRAINE *stops beating* FRANKIE *with the shoe.* FRANKIE *lets go of her. They all stare at* JAKE.*)*

LORRAINE: That boy's a maniac. Always has been. *(Pause)* What's he doin' now?

FRANKIE: He's out again. He goes in and out like that. All through the day. I don't know what's goin' on with him.

SALLY: He's crazy. He's just plain crazy.

LORRAINE: We gotta get him outa here. He's just goin' to seed in this dump. It's this place that's doin' it to him.

SALLY: We can't keep him at home, Mom.

LORRAINE: Why not? That's where he belongs. He belongs home.

SALLY: He's dangerous! That's why!

LORRAINE: He's dyin' here.

SALLY: He needs a doctor.

LORRAINE: He needs us is what he needs.

FRANKIE: If you could take him for a couple days, Mom, I could get back and find out what happened with Beth. You think you could do that? I just need a couple a' days. I gotta find out for sure what's goin' on.

LORRAINE: I'm gonna take him on a permanent basis. I'm not even gonna let him outa his room for a solid year. Maybe that'll teach him.

SALLY: What if he hurts somebody? He's liable to do anything in the state he's in.

LORRAINE: He's not gonna hurt us. We're related. Look at him. He's just a big baby. That's all he is. He's not gonna hurt us. Strangers he'll hurt. Strange women. Outsiders he'll hurt. That's guaranteed. But not us. He knows us.

SALLY: Mom, if you bring him in that house—I'm leavin'.

LORRAINE: Then leave, girl. This is my boy here.

(Blackout)

SCENE 6

Lights up left. BETH*'s bed upstage in very dim light, just able to make out her form lying with her face turned away from audience, almost the identical position and attitude of sleep as* JAKE *in previous scene. A small fold-out hospital screen in front of bed that can be seen through. The perimeters of the area are more fully lit, revealing* MIKE, *his mother,* MEG, *and his father,* BAYLOR, *downstage.*

BAYLOR: What do ya mean, "brain damage"? How can they prove somethin' like that?

MIKE: She had an X-ray, Dad. They're not sure how bad it is yet. She's having a lot of trouble talking.

BAYLOR: She gone crazy, or what?

MIKE: No. She's had an injury to the brain. You understand? Doesn't mean it's permanent. Doesn't mean she's crazy either.

BAYLOR: Well, what the hell does it mean then? "Injury to the brain" sounds like a permanent situation to me.

MEG: Oh my goodness. How in the world could a thing like this ever happen?

MIKE: I told you, Mom. Jake beat her up. He beat the shit out of her.

BAYLOR: Watch your language.

MEG: Who's Jake?

MIKE: Her husband, Mom. Jake.

28

MEG: Oh.

MIKE: You remember Jake, don't ya?

MEG: Wasn't he the son of those people we don't talk to anymore?

MIKE: Yeah. That's right.

BAYLOR: Bunch a' Okies. Don't surprise me one bit.

MEG: I think I do remember him.

MIKE: You were there at the wedding.

MEG: I was?

BAYLOR: I wasn't.

MIKE: *(To* BAYLOR*)* No, you stayed away. You made a point a' that.

BAYLOR: I was fishin'.

MEG: I think I do remember that. There was cars all over the place. Lots of cars. I kept wondering how come they had to park on the lawn. Why'd they have to do that?

MIKE: I don't know, Mom.

MEG: Wasn't there a parking lot or anything?

BAYLOR: Well, when're we gonna be able to see her?

MIKE: She's sleeping right now.

BAYLOR: Well, wake her up. We drove all the way down here from Billings just to see her. Now wake her up.

MIKE: I wish you'd have called me or something before you came down.

BAYLOR: Why should I call you?

MIKE: She's having a kind of a rough time right now, Dad. She needs a lot of rest.

BAYLOR: Listen, I got two mules settin' out there in the parkin' lot I gotta deliver by midnight. I'm supposed to be at the sale by six tomorrow mornin' and those mules have to be in the stalls by midnight tonight.

MIKE: You brought mules down here?

BAYLOR: Yeah. Why not? Might as well do a little business long as I'm gonna be down in this country anyway. That all right by you?

MEG: They made so much noise. I was so embarrassed once we hit the city. Felt like such a hick. There we are pulling mules in an open trailer and everyone's staring at us like we made a wrong turn or something.

BAYLOR: Looks like we did make a wrong turn if we can't even see our own daughter. What's the story here, anyway? They got her locked up or something?

MIKE: This is a hospital, Dad. They don't lock you up in a hospital.

BAYLOR: Oh, they don't huh.

MEG: They locked me up once, didn't they, Dad?

BAYLOR: That wasn't you. That was your mother.

MEG: Oh.

BAYLOR: That was a long time ago, anyhow.

MEG: It wasn't me?

MIKE: Maybe we could go down to the cafeteria and have some coffee or something. She might be awake by the time we get back.

BAYLOR: I ain't gonna drink any a' that damn hospital coffee. And I'm not talkin' to no doctors either. I wanna see my daughter!

MIKE: You don't have to talk to any doctors.

BAYLOR: I didn't come all the way down here to be made a fool of in front of a bunch a' college boys.

MIKE: Nobody's interested in making a fool out of you, Dad. Beth's sick. She needs attention. And everybody here is doing the best they can for her.

BAYLOR: Well, that sounds like ya don't need us then. Sounds like you got all the bases covered here. Come on, Meg, let's head back home then.

(BAYLOR *takes* MEG *by the elbow*)

MEG: Well, we just got here, didn't we?

BAYLOR: I gotta get those mules out to the fairgrounds. Now let's go.
We're wastin' our time here.

MIKE: Dad, wait a second. There's no reason to get offended.

BAYLOR: I'm not offended! What the hell, I'm just a dumb rancher.
What do I know? I don't know the first damn thing about "brain
damage." They got specialists for that. Ain't that right? They got
boys back there with diplomas tall as a man. What am I supposed to know about it?

MIKE: If you can just wait—if you can just stay for an hour or so—

BAYLOR: I can't wait. I got stock to feed. Now let's go, Meg.

MIKE: Well, then, let Mom stay with me. Beth needs to see her. I'll
bring her back home in a few days.

MEG: That would be nice.

(*Pause*)

BAYLOR: Where's she supposed to stay?

MIKE: She can stay with me.

BAYLOR: (*To* MIKE) How're you gonna watch out for her and your
sister both. That's more'n one man can handle. More'n two men
can handle.

MIKE: It's not that big a problem. They've got nurses here.

BAYLOR: You're gonna drive all the way back north with her? You're
gonna wanna do that? Bring her all the way back up north?

MIKE: Just let me worry about it, okay?

BAYLOR: Well, what am I supposed to do, talk to myself all the way
back home? That's a five-hundred-mile truck trip.

MEG: They got good radio between here and Billings, Dad.

BAYLOR: Good radio? All they got is that Eddie Jackrabbit. You call that music.

MEG: I liked it.

BAYLOR: All right. All right. *(To* MEG*)* You wanna stay?

MEG: I'd like to.

BAYLOR: All right. *(To* MIKE*)* How many days you think it'll be?

MIKE: Two or three.

MEG: I'll be fine, Baylor.

BAYLOR: You'll be fine. You'll be fine. Sure. All right. I'll go out and get your jacket out of the truck. Be right back.

MEG: I won't need it.

BAYLOR: *(As he exits)* You'll need it. You always need it.

*(*BAYLOR *exits.* MEG *turns and smiles at* MIKE.*)*

MEG: He's right.

*(*BETH *suddenly rolls over facing audience. Spotlight on her face. The rest of her body in dim light.)*

BETH: Mom?

(Blackout)

SCENE 7

Lights up upstage right. JAKE, *propped up with pillows, facing audience in a single bed that's now too short for him. He's in boxer underwear and a sleeveless T-shirt now and covered with an old Mexican blanket. Face even whiter than before, sunken eyes, hair slicked back as if he's just had a shower. Plastic model airplanes covered in dust and cobwebs of World War Two fighters and bombers hang from the ceiling directly above the bed.* LORRAINE *sits beside him on a chair stage left of bed, spoon-feeding him from a bowl of her cream of broccoli soup.* JAKE *refuses to eat.*

LORRAINE: *(Holding spoon of soup at his mouth)* Here now, come on. Just try a sip. That's all I'm askin'. Just a simple sip. I'm not askin' for the whole bowl. We'll work up to that slow. Just a little tiny old sip for now. Jake? *(Harder)* Sit up here and drink this soup! I'm sick of babyin' you. This is your favorite. Cream of broccoli. I made it special in the blender.

(Pause. JAKE *refuses soup.)*

I don't know why in the world you insist on gettin' so worked up over a woman. Look at you. I have never in my life seen you lookin' so let-down. You musta lost a good thirty, forty pounds. A woman ain't worth that kind of a loss. Believe you me. There's more pretty girls than one in this world. Not that she was such a looker. I can't even remember what she looked like to tell you the truth, but she couldn'ta been all that great. You'll find someone else sooner or later. You're a strong, strappin' man yet. Got a

33

little age on you now but that don't matter when you got a strong frame. Your daddy was still lookin' good at the age of sixty, even though the bottle had walked across his face a few times over. His face was a mess, I'll admit that. I'll be the first to admit that. But he still had that big stout frame on him, just like you got. Still managed to twirl my ticket, I'll tell ya that much. Somebody's bound to come along, just dyin' to be encircled by them big bony arms. Don't you worry about that one bit. Now, come on, just try this soup. Just do me a little favor, all right? Do you want me to play helicopter with it like we used to?

(She raises the spoon of soup over his head and starts making helicopter sounds as JAKE *watches the spoon from below.)*

LORRAINE: *(In a pinched cartoon voice)* Man overboard! Man overboard! Looks like he could be drownin'! Better lower down the life-support. Take it slow, we don't wanna lose him now.

*(*JAKE *suddenly knocks the spoon out of her hand and sends it flying. He rips the blanket and sheet off himself, grabs the bowl out of her hand, stands on the bed, holds the bowl high above his head and sends it crashing down on the mattress. Then he begins to stomp on the soup, jumping all over the bed, exhaling loudly and grunting like a buffalo.* LORRAINE *backs off fast and stands there watching him.* JAKE *finally expends all his energy and just stands there limply on the bed, bent forward at the waist, arms dangling and gasping for air.)*

LORRAINE: *(Away from him, keeping her distance)* What in the name of Judas Priest is the matter with you, boy! I spent hours makin' that stuff. I slaved over the blender tryin' to get it creamy and smooth, just how you like it! Look what you've done to that soup!

*(*JAKE *looks down at his feet, covered in soup. He just stares at his feet.)*

Look what you've done to your bed. *(She moves toward bed.)*

JAKE: *(Staying on bed)* STAY AWAY FROM MY BED!

*(*LORRAINE *stops. Pause. They stare at each other.)*

LORRAINE: You got everybody buffaloed, don't ya? Everybody's worried sick that you've gone off yer cake, but you don't fool me one bit. You scared your sister so damn bad she quit the house.

JAKE: Sally? Where'd she go?

LORRAINE: She left. I don't know where. Just packed up and left. Probably just as well.

JAKE: *(Still standing on bed)* She shouldn't a' left me! She'll regret that.

LORRAINE: Who wants to be around you, the way you act. Your brother's run off to God-knows-where, tryin' to hunt up that dingbat woman a' yours.

(JAKE gets off the bed fast, moves away from it, charges across stage as though he's going somewhere, then stops short.)

JAKE: Frankie? Where'd he go? Where is Frankie? I knew that would happen! Soon as I'm outa the picture.

(LORRAINE goes to bed and starts ripping the sheets and blanket off it, cleaning up the mess. JAKE moves around the space, lost.)

LORRAINE: He went back to wherever in the hell she's from. Montana or somethin'. Weren't they originally from Montana? I don't know. I can't keep track of it anymore.

JAKE: I told him not to go back there!

LORRAINE: What difference does it make?

JAKE: She's dead! I told him that already. She's dead!

LORRAINE: Just cool your britches down.

JAKE: He's got no business foolin' around in this thing! This was strictly between me and her. Where's my pants?

(He starts to search for his pants)

LORRAINE: You're not goin' anywhere. You're sick.

JAKE: Where's my goddamn pants! He's sneakin' behind my back. I gotta go catch him before he gets there.

LORRAINE: You can't go outside in your condition. You wouldn't last a day.

JAKE: I need my pants now! I NEED MY PANTS!

(JAKE *stops suddenly again, gasping for breath. He looks around the space, not seeming to recognize where he is. He stares at the model airplanes. Pause.*)

LORRAINE: Look at ya. You haven't got any wind to speak of. How're you gonna go out in the world like that?

JAKE: I can't stay here.

LORRAINE: Why not? You never should a' left in the first place. This was the first room you ever had to yourself.

JAKE: Where were we before?

LORRAINE: You mean, before here?

JAKE: Yeah. Before. Where were we before?

LORRAINE: You-Name-It-U.S.A. Those were the days we chased your daddy from one air base to the next. Always tryin' to catch up with the next "Secret Mission." Some secret. He was always cookin' up some weird code on the phone. Tryin' to make a big drama outa things. Thought it was romantic I guess. Worst of it was I fell for it. .

(JAKE *wanders around space, trying to recognize it.*)

JAKE: What code?

LORRAINE: Oh, I can't remember them now. There was lots of 'em. It was so many years ago. He'd make 'em all up.

JAKE: Why'd he use a code?

LORRAINE: He said it was because they didn't want him to reveal his location.

JAKE: Did you believe him?

LORRAINE: Yeah. Why shouldn't I of?

JAKE: Maybe he was lyin'.

LORRAINE: Why would he do that?

JAKE: So you wouldn't know what he was up to. That's why. Why do you think men lie to women?

LORRAINE: That was back when we were in love.

JAKE: Oh.

LORRAINE: That was back before things went to pieces.

JAKE: *(Still moving around space)* But we finally tracked him down, huh?

LORRAINE: Yeah. 'Course we tracked him down. Turned out not to be worth the trip, but we found him all right.

JAKE: Where?

LORRAINE: Different places. You were pretty little then.

JAKE: Little.

LORRAINE: Just a spit of a thing. I used to pack you to sleep in a dresser drawer. You were that tiny.

JAKE: You didn't close the drawer, did ya?

LORRAINE: No. 'Course not.

(JAKE stops and stares at her. Pause.)

JAKE: Where's that box?

LORRAINE: What?

JAKE: That box they put him in. You said you'd save that box for me. That little leather box.

LORRAINE: Oh—the ashes?

JAKE: Yeah.

LORRAINE: Now, how can you remember somethin' like that and not remember this room?

JAKE: Some things stick in your mind. Where's the box!

LORRAINE: It's here. It's right under the bed, there. You said save it, so I saved it.

JAKE: I wanna see the box.

LORRAINE: All right. Don't get so excited. It's right under here, unless the mice have gotten to it. I never looked at it again once I stuck it under here.

(She goes to bed, kneels down on floor and reaches under it. She digs around through various items under the bed.)

JAKE: How come you kept it under the bed?

LORRAINE: Couldn't figure out where else to put it. Couldn't stand lookin' at this stuff anymore and I was afraid to throw it away.

JAKE: How come?

LORRAINE: I don't know. Superstition, I guess.

(She pulls out a dusty American flag, folded in a triangle military-style. She hands it to him. JAKE takes it and stares at it.)

Here's the flag they gave you at the service. You remember that? Some government guy in dark glasses said a prayer over him and then he gave you that flag.

(She goes back to searching under the bed for the box as JAKE stares at the flag. He wipes the dust off it.)

JAKE: Dusty.

LORRAINE: *(As she searches under bed)* Yeah, well, like I said, I haven't touched a thing under here for years.

JAKE: You coulda dusted it off.

LORRAINE: Here it is.

(She pulls out a small leather box covered with dust. She blows the dust off the top and wipes it clean with the hem of her dress. She stands and hands the box to JAKE.)

I told ya I'd save it. 'Case you ever wanted it back someday.

JAKE: *(Holding box on top of flag)* This is him?

LORRAINE: What's left of him.

JAKE: *(Feeling weight of box)* He's kinda heavy.

LORRAINE: Well, he's a lot lighter than he was.

(LORRAINE picks the sheets and blanket back up off the floor.)

JAKE: Is this all that's left?

LORRAINE: Naw, there's a box a' medals and a leather flying jacket under there. More stuff in the garage. You can have it all. Take the whole kaboodle. I don't want it. Never did. I only saved it for you.

(JAKE moves to bed and sets the flag and box down on it, then he kneels down beside bed, reaches under and pulls out a cardboard carton full of Air Force medals and a leather flying jacket with small red bombs scratched into one of the sleeves. He sets the carton up on bed, then sits beside it and starts digging through the medals, holding them up to the light. LORRAINE watches him with her arms full of sheets.)

Jake, you can stay here as long as ya want to. I don't mind, really. I'm still your mother. You can just live in this room again. Just like you used to. I'll bring ya stuff. We can have conversations. Tell each other stories. You don't ever have to go outa this room again if you don't want to.

(JAKE stares up at the model airplanes, then down at the leather jacket. He puts the jacket on. He scratches at the red bombs on the sleeve. Pause.)

JAKE: How was it he died?

(Pause. They stare at each other.)

LORRAINE: Jake, you remember all that.

JAKE: No. I don't remember. I don't remember it at all.

LORRAINE: Jake—

JAKE: JUST TELL ME!

(Pause)

LORRAINE: He burned up.

JAKE: His plane crashed?

LORRAINE: No. He was no hero. Got hit by a truck. Drunk as a snake out in the middle of the highway. Truck blew up and he went with it. You already know that.

(JAKE leaps to his feet but stays by the bed.)

JAKE: DON'T TELL ME I ALREADY KNOW SOMETHIN' I DON'T KNOW! DON'T TELL ME THAT! HOW COULD I KNOW SOMETHIN' THAT I DON'T KNOW?

(Pause. They stare at each other.)

LORRAINE: *(Quietly)* Because you were there, Jake. You were right there with him when it happened.

(JAKE just stays there, staring at her. LORRAINE pulls the sheets up into a tight bundle, close to her.)

You just try and get some rest now, okay? I gotta go do this laundry. I'll be right out on the back porch if you need me. You just holler. Best thing you can do now is rest. Don't think about a thing, Jake. Just rest. Don't think about nothin'.

*(*LORRAINE *exits upstage, out of the light, carrying the sheets.* JAKE *stays in place, staring out across to stage left. Very softly light begins to come up on* BETH*'s hospital bed, now made up with blue satin sheets.* BETH *is alone, sitting on the upstage side of the bed with her back to* JAKE. *She is naked from the waist up with a blue silk dress pulled down around her waist and blue high heels with stockings. She is uninjured now—no bandage, her hair soft and beautiful. She is oiling her shoulders and chest from a small bottle beside her.* JAKE *just stares across at her as the light very slowly rises on her. She continues oiling herself slowly and seductively, unaware of* JAKE. *She is simply his vision. The light on her is continuously rising but remains very low.*

Suddenly JAKE *makes a move toward her and the light on her blacks out. She disappears. He stops short. Stares into the blackness, then turns and stares at his bed. All the rest of the lights black out except for a tight spotlight on his father's box of ashes.* JAKE *crosses back to the box, picks it up, opens it and stares into it for a second. He blows lightly into the box, sending a soft puff of ashes up into the beam of the spotlight. Spotlight fades slowly to black.)*

Act II

SCENE 1

Lights up, stage-left set. Living room in BETH'*s* PARENTS' *house. Same black platform as Act I but now two walls are flown in, stage left and upstage. The upstage wall has a swinging kitchen door mounted to stage right and an open hallway entrance to stage left, with no door, that leads off to an upstairs bedroom. The space visible through open hallway entrance is black and void. Same with space seen through kitchen door when it swings open. A small porch landing with three steps and a handrail is added onto the down-right corner of platform. A window with curtains, dead center of stage-left wall, with black void again seen through window. A well-worn sofa sits under the window, stage left, angled slightly toward audience. A stuffed armchair upstage of sofa, facing audience. An old-fashioned stand-up reading lamp between armchair and sofa. An oval rag rug on floor in front of sofa. A wooden gun rack center of upstage wall. Nothing else. The impression should be very simple and stark yet maintain a sense of realism. If wallpaper is used, it should be subdued and very faded.*

   BETH *is sitting on edge of sofa dressed in one of* BAYLOR'*s faded red plaid shirts, way too big for her. It hangs outside her jeans, to the knees. Bare feet. No bandage now. Short hair. Her bruises almost healed up.* MEG *approaches her, entering through kitchen door, with a pair of fuzzy slippers in one hand and a pair of heavy work boots in the other. Before lights rise, the sound of a dog defending his territory is heard in the distance off right. Two distant voices of men arguing. The words unintelligible.*

MEG: Here we go, honey. I've got slippers or boots. Warm, fuzzy slippers. How 'bout these? They're very kind to the skin. Like having little lambs wrapped around your toes.

BETH: *(Distracted by outdoor sounds)* No, my feet are fine. I like them fine. Naked. They can move.

MEG: But the floor's so cold. This time a' year the floor's cold as ice. I used to even put socks on the dogs when they came in. Then your father put a stop to that, of course.

BETH: *(Standing, looks toward direction of voices)* Where—who's out there?

MEG: Outside? I don't know, honey. Mike wouldn't tell me.

BETH: Mike? Heez out there?

MEG: Yes. He's been out there all morning talking to that man.

BETH: *(Moving downstage to porch, looking out)* What man?

MEG: Some man. I don't know. He just showed up.

BETH: Whatz his voice?

MEG: What, honey?

BETH: Whatz his voice? Someone I know. Iz voice I know.

MEG: I couldn't see him from the front door. Mike wouldn't let him come up to the house.

BETH: *(Turns fast to MEG)* Who'ze—who'ze?

MEG: Don't you wanna try these slippers, honey? They'd keep you nice and cozy.

BETH: Tha's a voice of someone. Before. Someone with a voice before. Someone—I know.

MEG: I'm not sure who it is. Mike doesn't like him, that's for sure. I just wish he'd go away so the dog would quit.

BETH: *(Moving back toward sofa)* Someone with Jake. Jake's voice. Iz—a man with hiz voice. Same. Heez come to see me? Haz he come to see me?

(The sounds outside stop.)

MEG: Honey, I can't ask Mike. You know how he gets. He gets just like your father. There's no point in asking.

BETH: I—I—can I go? Can I go out to see? I want to see. Can I?

MEG: No, honey. It's freezing out there. The ground's solid ice.

BETH: He can't go. He can't. Don't let him go. I want to see.

MEG: Honey, it's nothing but a man. A stranger. Some stranger.

(MIKE *enters fast from upstage center space, moves down to stairs and enters from porch. He's in a heavy jacket, gloves, wool cap, boots with snow on them; carries shotgun. He unloads shotgun and sets it on gun rack upstage wall, stomps his boots and takes his gloves and jacket off.)*

Oh, we were just now talking about you, Mike. I thought you were down by the road.

MIKE: Son of a bitch wanted to come right up to the goddamn house. Can you believe that? Walk right up to the house like a neighbor or somethin'. I can't believe it. Who do these guys think they are, anyway?

MEG: Don't swear in the house, Mike. I've told you that since you were a little boy. Keep the language outdoors.

BETH: *(To Mike)* Who'ze he? Who'ze he?

MIKE: Nobody. Just—just a guy. I don't know.

BETH: Jake?

MIKE: *(Turning on BETH)* No!! It's not Jake! All right? He's got nothin' to do with Jake. Just some guy. When're you gonna stop thinkin' about Jake for Christ's sake!

BETH: You lie to me! You lie like I'm dead. I'm not dead.

MIKE: Oh, so now you're *not* dead. Today you're not dead. Yesterday you were dead but today you're not. I gotta keep track a' this. Makes a big difference who you're talkin' to—a corpse or a live person.

MEG: Please don't yell in the house. The walls can't take it.

BETH: I'm not the one who's dead.

MIKE: *(To* BETH*)* You just settle down, all right! You just settle down now. I've about had it with you. I've been out there all night long in zero cold tryin' to protect you!

BETH: You're not the guard of me!

MIKE: Well, who is then? Who's gonna protect you? I'm the only one left around here.

MEG: There is no reason to scream. Screaming is not the thing we're born for.

(Pause)

BETH: Haz he gone now?

MIKE: Yeah. Yeah, he's gone.

(Pause)

BETH: *(To* MIKE*)* You—you. You don' let me come back. Why don' you let me come back?

MIKE: *(Moves toward her)* Beth—

BETH: *(Stiffens, stands back)* No! You make—you make a war. You make a war. You make an enemy. In me. In me! An enemy. You. You. You think me. You think you know. You think. You have a big idea.

MIKE: I'm just trying to keep you out of trouble. Can't you get that in your head? I'm tired of going through this with you.

BETH: You—you have a feeling. You have a feeling I'm you. I'm not you! This! *(Points to her head.)* This didn't happen to you. This! This. This thought. You don't know this thought. How? How can you know this thought? In me.

MEG: Beth, your brother's only trying to help you. He's only doing what he thinks best. Now don't get so excited. You'll only get yourself all worked up again.

BETH: *(To MEG, softens)* You—you a love. You—you are only that. Only. You don' know. Only love. Good. You. Mother. You. Always love. Always. *(To MIKE)* But he lies to me. Like I'm gone. Not here. Lies and tellz me iz for love. Iz not for love! Iz pride!

MIKE: Okay. Okay, I'll tell you exactly the truth. I'll tell you. You wanna know? It was Jake's brother. Okay? That's who it was. Jake's little lousy brother.

BETH: Jake?

MIKE: HIS BROTHER! NOT JAKE! HIS BROTHER!

MEG: Mike!

MIKE: *(To MEG)* Well, goddamnit! She wants to know the truth. She says—"tell me the truth, you're lying to me." I tell her the truth and she turns it into a lie. I'm sick and tired of this shit. *(To BETH)* What do you wanna know? You want me to tell you it was Jake? Okay, it was Jake. How's that? You're gonna believe whatever you want to anyway. What do you wanna believe?

BETH: It was not Jake.

MIKE: It was his brother! His pathetic little brother. Sniveling up here to our doorstep, asking for forgiveness.

BETH: Why'z he gone?

MIKE: What'd you expect me to do? Huh? Did you want me to invite him in for hot chocolate or something? Cookies? Pretend nothing ever happened? He's just on a friendly visit? Sometimes I think you must've enjoyed getting beat up. Maybe that's it. Maybe you get some kind of kick out of it.

(Pause)

MEG: You don't need to be cruel, Mike.

MIKE: This whole thing is cruel.

(Long pause as BETH *stares at her shirt, touches the sleeves. Her whole tone shifts.)*

BETH: What's this shirt?

MEG: That's Baylor's, honey. You wanted that one. That's the one you picked out of the closet.

BETH: Smells like him. Baylor.

MEG: He used to always wear that fishing. That was his favorite shirt. He said you could have it.

BETH: Smells like fish.

MIKE: So, now what? We're gonna talk about shirts now? *(To* BETH*)* What is goin' on with you? You shift streams faster than a trout in heat.

BETH: *(Soft, to* MIKE*)* If something breaks—broken. If something broken—parts still—stay. Parts still float. For a while. Then gone. Maybe never come—back. Together. Maybe never.

(Sound of single shot from a deer rifle in distance stage right.)

*(*BETH*'s head jerks toward sound.)*

Zaat?

MIKE: Dad. Hunting.

MEG: He's been out there all night again. I just don't understand how he can take the cold like that. Sometimes I think he'd rather live out there in that hunting shack year-round. He's got everything he needs out there. His magazines. His flashlight. His radio. He even eats his meals out there, anymore. I don't know when all that started.

MIKE: All what?

MEG: Him moving out. When did that start?

MIKE: He hasn't moved out. He's hunting. Every year he hunts. You know that.

MEG: Sometimes I think he's hiding from us.

(Pause. MIKE *goes to armchair, sits, takes his boots off and stretches his legs out—continuous as he speaks.)*

MIKE: Well, there's only one day left in the season and he hasn't got his buck yet.

MEG: I don't know if I can take another winter of venison. Last year we had venison three times a day. Venison, venison, venison. It still wasn't gone by spring. God, how I hate that meat. Even bacon can't hide the taste.

MIKE: It's not that bad if you don't smell it.

MEG: Funny thing is, I don't think he likes the meat either. He never eats it. Poor excuse for killing a live thing if you ask me.

BETH: *(Staring around at space)* This—this—this is where I used to be?

MEG: Where, honey?

BETH: Here? Inside here. This room?

MEG: Yes. This is our home. You recognize it, don't you?

BETH: This room was—where we all were—together.

MEG: Yes. That's right. Christmas, Thanksgiving, Easter. We were always here.

MIKE: You're safe here. Long as you stay with us.

BETH: What's "safe"?

MIKE: Safe. Safe from injury. You won't get hurt here.

BETH: I hurt all over.

MEG: But it's getting better, honey. Every day it's getting a little bit better.

BETH: What is?

MEG: The brain. They say the brain heals itself just like the skin. Isn't that amazing? It just keeps healing itself. That's what they told us at the hospital.

BETH: What brain?

MEG: Your brain, honey.

BETH: Where? In me.

MIKE: In your head. The brain in your head. Inside your skull.

BETH: Iz hiding in there?

MEG: No, I woudn't say that exactly. The brain can't hide.

BETH: Iz in there like a turtle? Like a shell?

MEG: Not really. It's—what does a brain look like, Mike?

MIKE: It don't know what it looks like. It's gray. That's about all I know about it.

MEG: Yes. It's a gray thing. Kind of like a snail, isn't it, Mike? It's kind of curled around itself like a big snail.

MIKE: You got me.

BETH: Snail.

MEG: Yes. I think so. I't all lumpy. I saw pictures of it once. They took pictures of my mother's brain. They showed them to me once.

BETH: We can't see it?

MIKE: Not when you're alive. You can't see it when you're alive.

BETH: Why?

MIKE: Because—you'd be dead if you could see it. It'd be sticking out.

BETH: You can see the head? The face.

MIKE: Yeah. That's right. But not the brain. The brain's inside the head. Covered up.

BETH: Where?

MIKE: *(Slaps his forehead)* Inside! Here! Inside! Behind the skull!

(BAYLOR's VOICE heard offstage.)

BAYLOR: *(Offstage)* Just try to keep your weight off it. That's it. Don't put yer weight down on it. Hang on. Just keep ahold of my neck now.

(BAYLOR enters from upstage, then up porch stairs, wearing hunter's orange from head to toe and a camouflage hunting vest, rifle in one hand. He helps FRANKIE on stage, who is hopping on his right leg, arm around BAYLOR's neck, a hole about the size of a quarter in his left thigh with a little patch of blood—nothing more. As they enter, MIKE immediately gets up and grabs his shotgun, sticks the shells back in it and snaps the barrels shut. BAYLOR assists FRANKIE over to the sofa. FRANKIE collapses onto sofa holding his left thigh in pain.)

MEG: Oh, my goodness, Baylor. What in the world happened here? We heard you shooting.

BAYLOR: Aw, this yayhoo was out there in the damn woods without a lick a' orange on him. Came crashing through that stand of aspen like a freight train and I shot him.

MEG: You shot him? Oh, my God, Baylor.

BAYLOR: Nailed him clean through the thigh. Look at that. Bullet passed right on through and out the other side. Never touched the bone or nothin'.

MEG: *(To Frankie)* But it still must hurt. Doesn't it hurt?

FRANKIE: Yeah. It hurts.

MEG: It must.

BAYLOR: Hurts me too. Wrecked my entire day a' shootin'. I got one day left to bag my limit and this bonehead comes along and scares every damn deer in four counties.

FRANKIE: I'm sorry. I was looking for my car.

BAYLOR: Your car? Where'd you park it, in the lake?

MEG: Oh, my goodness.

BAYLOR: Stop staying "Oh, my goodness, Oh my God," all the time. Think up somethin' different for a change.

MIKE: *(Approaching* FRANKIE*)* You were tryin' to circle back around, weren't you? Isn't that what you were doin'? Thought you'd come up around the back side? I thought I told you to take a hike, buddy.

FRANKIE: *(Staring at* BETH*)* I just wanted to see her. That's all. All I wanna do is see her. *(To* BETH*)* My brother thinks you're dead, see. I gotta go back and tell him now.

BETH: Before—you. I know you. We—

MIKE: Beth, you go on up to the bedroom now. Go on!

BAYLOR: Aw, let her talk to him. Christ. What difference does it make now. He's not gonna do much harm with that hole in his leg. Mother, help me off with these boots.

*(*BAYLOR *sits heavily in armchair.* MEG *kneels in front of him and helps pull his boots off.)*

MIKE: I'll give him a ride down to the emergency.

BETH: No—he—he can stay. I know him.

MIKE: He's not stayin' in this house! I'll tell you that right now!

BAYLOR: *(To* MIKE*)* You keep yer voice down, boy! You forget whose house this is. *(Pause)* No point in movin' him around right now. Long as the blood's stopped. Best to prop that leg up and let him set for a while.

MEG: *(Stands, to* FRANKIE*)* I'll get something to put your foot on.

BAYLOR: *(To* MEG*)* Let Beth get it! You help me off with this gear now. I've never seen anybody get so easily distracted as you. Just keep yer mind on yer business now.

(MEG *kneels again in front of* BAYLOR, *finishes with his boots and starts pulling off his orange outer pants, as* BAYLOR *pulls them down from his waist. Underneath he's wearing heavy dungarees.*)

MEG: *(As she helps* BAYLOR*)* Beth, go get that little footstool out of the kitchen for the man.

BETH: Kitchen.

MEG: Yes. In the kitchen, honey. The little footstool. Bring it in here for him.

(BETH *exits through kitchen door upstage.*)

MIKE: *(As he puts his jacket, cap and gloves back on)* I got an idea. Why don't we just move him on up to the bedroom. Huh? We got an extra bedroom empty don't we? Let's just move him up there. Then we can serve him breakfast in bed. We can move the TV up there for him. How 'bout that? We can get the electric blanket. He could even share the room with Beth, maybe. That'd be nice and cozy.

BAYLOR: *(To* MIKE*)* Hey! You just cool yourself down, buster.

MIKE: I'm not stayin' in the same house with the brother of the man who tried to kill my sister! I'm not doin' that.

BAYLOR: I'm the one who shot him! All right? Since I'm the one who shot him, I'm gonna see to it that he stays alive. I'm too old to go to jail just yet. Thank you very much.

MEG: *(Still helping* BAYLOR *undress)* Can't we just talk in a normal tone?

BAYLOR: Soon's it gets normal we'll talk normal!

MIKE: *(Moving toward porch)* You just lemme know. You lemme know when he's outa here.

BAYLOR: Where you goin'?

MIKE: Out to the shack.

BAYLOR: *(To* MIKE*)* Wait a second. Take the 30-30. You see any deer out there, let 'em have it. There's only one day left.

MEG: *(To* MIKE*)* Just try not to shoot any more people please.

(BAYLOR *reaches for deer rifle, across* MEG, *and hands it to* MIKE. MIKE *takes it. He stares at* FRANKIE.)

MIKE: *(To* FRANKIE*)* You wormed your way in, didn't you? Pretty cute. But I'm not forgettin' anything. Everybody else might forget but I'm not. Far as I'm concerned you and your brother are the same person.

(MIKE *leans the shotgun against the sofa, then snaps the lever on the 30-30 and engages a bullet. He stares at* FRANKIE, *then exits out porch and upstage into blackness.)*

BAYLOR: *(To* MIKE *as he exits)* Don't mess that shack up. I spent all afternoon sweepin' the mouse shit out of it.

MEG: You shouldn't oughta make him go out in that cold, Baylor.

BAYLOR: Wasn't my idea. It's his.

(BETH *enters from kitchen door upstage with small footstool. She crosses fast downstage and just stands there, holding it. She stares at audience. Pause.)*

Well, take it on over to the man, Beth. Take it over and set it down for him. Don't just stand there with it. Not gonna do him any good while it's in the air.

MEG: *(Stands to help* BETH*)* Here, honey, I'll take it.

BAYLOR: No! *(Stops* MEG*)* Let her do it. She can do it. 'Bout time she starts doin' things by herself. You keep babyin' her she's never gonna get any better.

(BETH *stays in same place, holding stool. She turns and stares at* FRANKIE. MEG *kneels and goes back to helping* BAYLOR.)

BAYLOR: *(Deliberate)* Beth—take the stool over to the man and set it down for him. What're you starin' at?

(Pause. BETH *moves slowly over to* FRANKIE *and stops in front of him but keeps holding stool. She stares at* FRANKIE.*)*

BAYLOR: *(To* BETH*)* That's right. Now set it down on the floor. Right in front of him.

*(*BETH *sets the stool down on floor in front of* FRANKIE.*)*

That's the ticket. Now help him get his leg up on it.

FRANKIE: That's all right. I can do it.

*(*FRANKIE *struggles to get his leg up on stool but can't do it.)*

BAYLOR: *(To* FRANKIE*)* She can help you. Good for her to help somebody else out for a change. Make her realize she's not the only cripple in this world.

MEG: Baylor—

BAYLOR: *(To* MEG*)* What? She knows all about it. She knows somethin's gone wrong.

MEG: I know but you don't have to—

BAYLOR: What? Speak the plain truth? Everybody's been tiptoeing around here like she can't handle the plain truth. And she knows all about it. Don't ya, Beth?

*(*BETH *helps* FRANKIE *get his injured leg propped up on the stool.)*

FRANKIE: Thanks.

BAYLOR: *(To* MEG*)* There now. See that? Now she's got the experience of helping somebody else out. And you woulda robbed her a' that, see. You wanna just keep on lettin' her believe that she's never gonna pull outa this thing.

MEG: That's not true.

BAYLOR: That's good, Beth. Now why don't you go on in the kitchen and make us up a nice big pot a' black coffee.

MEG: She can't make coffee, Baylor. She'll burn herself.

BAYLOR: See, there ya go again.

MEG: Well, why take the risk of her getting hurt? She can't make coffee.

BAYLOR: That's right. "Why take the risk?" Why take the risk of her getting better? Why not just let her stay the same?

MEG: She is getting better.

BAYLOR: Nah. We'll be right back in the same boat we were in with your mother. Another invalid. House full a' invalids. I'll be the only one left in this joint that can function.

MEG: Well, you're never around anyway.

BAYLOR: I'm around. I'm around plenty. But I'll tell ya one thing—I'm not gonna be the caretaker of a nursing home here. I got better things to do.

MEG: Like shooting men.

BAYLOR: That was an accident.

MEG: Well, I don't understand how a man can be mistaken for a deer. They don't look anything alike.

BAYLOR: He was crashin' through the woods, hell bent for leather. How was I supposed to know?

MEG: Didn't you look? He doesn't have antlers or anything. He doesn't look anything like a deer.

BAYLOR: You don't make an examination before you shoot somethin'. You just shoot it.

FRANKIE: It was my fault.

BAYLOR: Yer darn tootin' it was your fault. Yer just lucky I'm as old as I am. In my prime you'da been dead meat, son.

BETH: *(To FRANKIE)* You have voice I know.

(Pause)

FRANKIE: 'Scuse me?

BETH: You have voice.

BAYLOR: *(To* FRANKIE*)* You understand what's happened to her, don't ya?

MEG: Baylor, please—

BAYLOR: *(To* MEG*)* Aw, knock it off. What in the hell are we tryin' to pull here? Beth, you go ahead and tell him. Go ahead. Tell the man what happened to you. Go on.

(Pause)

BETH: I—

FRANKIE: That's all right. I just mainly wanted to know if you were alive. My brother's worried sick about you. He said to tell you he just misses you a lot.

(Pause. Silence MEG *stands.)*

MEG: Maybe I'll make that pot of coffee, Baylor.

BAYLOR: All right. Why not. And bring me in that tin of Mink Oil for my feet. They're startin' to crack again.

MEG: Do you want to come in and help me, Beth?

*(*BETH *shakes her head, "no.")*

BAYLOR: *(To* MEG*)* Leave her be!

*(*MEG *exits through door upstage.* BETH *stands there staring at* FRANKIE. BAYLOR *stays in armchair.)*

BAYLOR: *(To* FRANKIE*)* Christ, there's gotta be a borderline between polite and stupid. I swear to God. Her mother was the same way. Drive you crazy with politeness. *(Pause. To* FRANKIE*)* How's that leg doin'?

FRANKIE: It just burns a little.

BAYLOR: I'll bet it does. You took a helluva lick.

BETH: *(Very simple to* FRANKIE*)* This—this is my father. He's given up
love. Love is dead for him. My mother is dead for him. Things
live for him to be killed. Only death counts for him. Nothing else.
This—This—*(She moves slowly toward* FRANKIE.*)* This is me. This
is me now. The way I am. Now. This. All. Different. I—I live
inside this. Remember. Remembering. You. You—were one. I
know you. I know—love. I know what love is. I can never forget.
That. Never.

(Lights fade. All three stay in place. Lights to black.)

SCENE 2

*Sound of electric shaver in darkness, stage right. Lights up slowly (cross fade with Scene 1 ending), on stage-right bedroom set—*JAKE's *bed with model airplanes above. Walls in.* JAKE *is standing extreme downstage on the very edge of the stage, facing audience, stage right of center. He is in his boxer shorts underwear, sleeveless T-shirt under his father's leather pilot's jacket. The jacket is covered with all the medals from the cardboard box now. He wears the American flag from his dad's funeral draped around his neck. He is shaving his face with a cordless electric shaver, staring straight in front of him as though there were a mirror. His face is pale white, eyes sunken. Lights up full. He finishes shaving. Shuts off shaver. Takes the cap off it and blows the whiskers out then replaces cap and stares in "mirror". He speaks to himself in a loud whisper as he looks at his face in the imaginary mirror.*

JAKE: *(Whisper)* Don't think about her feet or her calves or her knees or her thighs or her hips or her waist or her ribs or her tits or her armpits or her shoulders or her neck or her face or her eyes or her hair or her lips. Especially not her lips. Don't think about any of these things. You'll be much better off.

(He turns upstage just as SALLY *enters through up left door, wearing a jacket, jeans and western boots and carrying a suitcase. They both stop and stare at each other. Pause.* SALLY *closes the door, then turns back to* JAKE. *She keeps hold of the suitcase.)*

SALLY: How're you feelin', Jake?

58

JAKE: Me?

(Pause. He moves fast to the bed, pulls the flag off his neck as he crosses, kneels down beside bed, stuffs the flag under bed, pulls out a small black toilet case, unzips it, puts the shaver inside, zips it back up and shoves it back under the bed. He rises to his feet, then sits on the edge of the bed, facing SALLY, and rubs his knee as he stares at her. Pause.)

SALLY: *(Sets suitcase on floor)* Where's Mom?

JAKE: *(Rapid speech)* I don't worry anymore where anybody is. I don't think about that. Anybody can move wherever they want. I just try to keep track of my own movements these days. That's enough. Have you ever tried that? To follow yourself around? Like a spy. You can wind up anywhere. It's amazing. Like, just now I caught myself shaving. I was right over there. Shaving my face. I didn't know I was doing that until just now. It's kinda scary, ya know.

SALLY: Scary?

JAKE: Yeah. I mean there's a possibility that you could do something that you didn't even know about. You could be somewhere that you couldn't even remember being. Has that ever happened to you?

SALLY: No. No, it's the opposite with me. Everything just keeps repeating itself.

JAKE: Oh. Well, then you don't know what I'm talkin' about.

(Pause. She stares at him. He grabs his knees and stares at the floor.)

SALLY: Um—I decided to come back and see if I could maybe help you out, Jake. You don't mind, do ya?

JAKE: Me? Help me out?

(He gets off the bed fast, as though he's just remembered something important. He kneels down on floor again, pulls toilet case out, unzips it, digs around in case and pulls out a toenail clipper. He zips case back up

and shoves it under bed. Then he sits on edge of bed, facing SALLY, *and starts clipping his toenails.* SALLY *just stands there watching him, stuffs her hands in her pockets.)*

SALLY: I was out there—I was driving around in the car out there and—

JAKE: Where were you headed?

SALLY: I was just—I was driving around the house. In circles. Real slow. I couldn't make up my mind.

JAKE: No, I mean where were you headed originally? Before you decided to come back?

SALLY: I wasn't sure. I mean—I was thinkin'—at first I was thinkin' I'd go up and try to see Beth, and then—

*(*JAKE *stands suddenly. Starts moving around the room.* SALLY *just stands there.)*

JAKE: Beth? You were gonna' go and try to see Beth? Nobody believes me!

SALLY: Now wait a second—

JAKE: NOBODY BELIEVES ME! Bunch a' traitors for family. Did you talk to Frankie about her before you left?

SALLY: No! Why would I talk to Frankie?

JAKE: You're a liar. You wouldn't have thought to go see her unless you'd talked to Frankie first. Why would you think to go see her? She's dead! Didn't I tell ya that already?

SALLY: Yeah. But I thought I'd go see her anyway.

JAKE: A dead person? You wanted to go see a dead person?

SALLY: There was other times when you said you'd killed her—when you thought you'd killed her—remember?

*(*JAKE *stops, stares at her. Pause.)*

JAKE: So what'd you come back here for?

SALLY: I don't know exactly. I started thinkin' about this whole thing. This family. How everything's kinda—shattered now.

JAKE: Now? What d'ya mean "now"? When wasn't it shattered?

SALLY: I don't wanna start fightin' with you just when I walk in the door. I didn't come back for that.

JAKE: *(Crossing back to bed)* Why not? What else are we gonna' do? Huh? You got some brave ideas? You got some brave ideas about mending things up. Is that it? I'll tell ya the only idea that's gonna work. I been sittin' here in this room for days thinkin' about it and I finally came up with it.

SALLY: What's that.

JAKE: *(Sits on bed, quieter)* I'm not goin' outdoors anymore. I'm not leavin' this room. Mom brings me food. I don't need the outside. All I do is get in trouble out there.

SALLY: Well, you can't just stay locked up in here, Jake. That's crazy.

JAKE: No. Out there is crazy. Out there. Soon's you step out that door.

(JAKE goes back to clipping his toenails again. He ignores her. Pause. SALLY watches him. Pause.)

SALLY: *(Turning toward her suitcase)* All right. I guess I was wrong. I thought there might be a chance I could talk to you and see if we could be friends or somethin', but I guess I was dead wrong.

JAKE: Wait a second, Sally. Come on.

SALLY: Naw, you make it impossible. You're gonna sit around here pretending to be crazy. Tryin' to make everyone believe you're crazy. Is that what you're gonna do? Well, it's not gonna change what you did. You already got away with that once, didn't you?

JAKE: Sally—

SALLY: Don't worry. I'm not gonna give you away.

JAKE: We made a promise.

SALLY: Yeah.

JAKE: Don't forget.

(Pause)

SALLY: I won't.

JAKE: Look, I need an ally. Just one. Just one good, solid ally that I can rely on. Everyone else is against me.

SALLY: No! I'm not doin' that again for you. Never again.

JAKE: *(Suddenly in a whisper)* Frankie called here. He called here. I heard Mom talkin' to him on the phone.

(Pause. SALLY stares at him. She sets suitcase down.)

SALLY: So what if Frankie called? Why shouldn't he call? He's your brother.

JAKE: *(Whisper)* He didn't ask to talk to me!

SALLY: Why are you whispering now? What's gotten into you?

JAKE: *(Whisper)* Mom.

SALLY: What about her?

JAKE: *(Whisper)* She's with him. Her and Frankie are together. They've got a pact.

SALLY: What're you talkin' about?

JAKE: *(Whisper)* They're tryin' to make me believe that Beth's alive.

SALLY: She probably is.

JAKE: Are you with them too?

SALLY: I'm not with anybody, all right! I'm all by myself.

JAKE: Then you can help me. There's no reason why you couldn't help me.

SALLY: Look, I went through this once with you, Jake. With Dad. I already went through this.

JAKE: *(Moving to her, pleading, in a whisper)* No, no, no. It's not the same. They wanna make me suffer. Don't you know that? Frankie thinks I deserve to suffer. So does Mom.

SALLY: Nobody wants to make you suffer. It's just you.

JAKE: *(Whisper)* It's that whole family too. Beth's family. You remember how they hated me.

SALLY: Will you please stop whispering! It's makin' me nuts!

(Pause. JAKE *stops and stares at her.)*

JAKE: *(Normal voice now)* You're afraid a' me, aren't ya? *(Pause)* Aren't ya!

SALLY: I'm not afraid of you.

JAKE: Yeah, you are.

SALLY: Only because you remind me of Dad sometimes.

JAKE: Dad? *(Pause)* Dad?

SALLY: Yeah. You do. Sometimes you sound just like him.

JAKE: I don't sound anything like him. I never sounded like him. I've made a point not to.

SALLY: You do. The way you get that creepy thing in your voice.

JAKE: What creepy thing?

SALLY: That high-pitched creepy thing like you're gonna turn into an animal or something.

JAKE: What animal?

SALLY: I don't know what animal!

JAKE: What kind of animal?

SALLY: Not any special kind. Just an animal sound in general.

(Pause. They stare at each other.)

JAKE: A bear?

SALLY: Don't get cute.

JAKE: You remember how he used to try to dance with you when he was drunk? How he'd pull you right up tight against his chest and breathe into your neck. You remember all that?

SALLY: What're you tryin' to do?

JAKE: He'd put on Lefty Frizell and twirl you around the kitchen until you got so dizzy you had to run into the bathroom and puke. I remember lyin' awake listening to you with the dry heaves and listening to him bellowing down the hallway at Mom. Warning her not to go in and help you out. I remember all that!

SALLY: Yeah! Then you remember the night he died too, don't ya?

(JAKE stops. They stare at each other. Pause.)

JAKE: No! *(Pause)* That's the part I forgot.

(LORRAINE enters quickly with a metal serving tray and wearing an apron. She stops when she sees SALLY. Pause.)

LORRAINE: *(To SALLY)* Oh. I thought you might've come back. I saw that car out there and I said to myself: "I bet she's back."

SALLY: That's pretty sharp, Mom.

LORRAINE: Just puttin' two and two together. *(Crosses to bed and starts putting the dirty breakfast dishes on tray.)* What'sa matter, you get homesick or somethin'? Don't tell me you got homesick for yer little ole family. Out there all alone on the big bad American road.

SALLY: Not exactly. No.

LORRAINE: Well, what was it then? You forget somethin'?

JAKE: *(To LORRAINE)* Were you listening to us out there?

LORRAINE: Out where?

JAKE: Outside the door! Were you out there, breathing on the door-knob, listening to us?

LORRAINE: Why? Have you all got some big terrible secret or somethin'? Talkin' behind my back again probably. Don't take long for the conspiracy to start, does it?

JAKE: You were, weren't you? *(To* SALLY*)* See, that's what I mean.

LORRAINE: What's what you mean?

JAKE: *(To* LORRAINE*)* I'm talkin' to her!

SALLY: *(To* LORRAINE*)* He thinks you and Frankie are in cahoots against him.

JAKE: *(To* SALLY*)* Don't tell her that!

SALLY: Why not? That's what you told me, isn't it?

JAKE: I didn't tell you that so you could tell her! That was private.

LORRAINE: So there *is* a secret.

SALLY: *(To* LORRAINE*)* He thinks you've got some kind of a plot going to make him suffer.

JAKE: Sally, you shut up!

LORRAINE: Suffer?

JAKE: I didn't say anything like that.

> *(*JAKE *stops. Pause.* JAKE *and* SALLY *look up and stare at each other like two dogs with their hackles up.* LORRAINE *watches them but continues to slowly collect the breakfast plates off the bed.)*

LORRAINE: Well—looks like you're just gonna have to stay away for a spell, Sally. We can't have him gettin' upset like this. Not in his condition. He wasn't like this until you showed up.

SALLY: *(Still with her eyes on* JAKE*)* I'm not leavin'. I'm sick to death of leavin'. Every time I pack, I tremble now. I start to tremble. It's in my body. My whole body shakes from the memory of all this leavin'. It feels like a leaving that will last forever. This is my home as much as his.

LORRAINE: But we're in a state of emergency here now, with your brother like this. This is a crisis. You have to be a little flexible in a crisis.

SALLY: I'm not leavin'!

LORRAINE: How can you be so mule-headed stubborn and selfish!

JAKE: *(To* LORRAINE, *moving away from* SALLY*)* She can stay if she wants to.

(Pause)

LORRAINE: There's not enough room, Jake.

JAKE: There's room. This is my room and she can stay if she wants to.

(Pause)

LORRAINE: Well this isn't gonna' be much fun, is it?

JAKE: *(To* LORRAINE*)* I want Sally here, where I can see her. Where I can keep an eye on her. She's not gonna be sending any messages for you anymore.

LORRAINE: Messages?

JAKE: Yeah, that's right. You can tell Frankie that she's not coming back there. She's staying with me. There's not gonna be any more codes sent.

LORRAINE: *(To* SALLY*)* What kinda trash have you been puttin' in his head?

JAKE: I'm just bein' careful, that's all. I want you to stay here. Right here in this room, Sally.

SALLY: Just like old times, huh? Okay. Okay. I will. Maybe that's just what I need to do. Take the tiger by the tail. I'll stay right in here with you. We'll just camp out.

LORRAINE: Well, I'm not doin' the cookin' anymore. I'll tell ya that much. I'm not runnin' a boardinghouse here.

SALLY: I'll cook.

LORRAINE: (Moves to SALLY) Why can't you just leave! Why can't you just get your fanny out in the wide world and find yourself somethin' to do. Stop mopin' around here gettin' everybody's dander up.

SALLY: Where do you want me to wind up, Mom? Somewhere down the road?

LORRAINE: You'll find somethin'. Everybody finds somethin' sooner or later.

SALLY: Like what?

LORRAINE: A town or somethin'.

SALLY: What town?

LORRAINE: I don't know what town! There's lots of towns around. This is a country full a' towns. There's a town for everybody. Always has been. If there's no town, then start one of your own. My granddaddy started a town on a mesquite stump. He just hung his hat on it and a whole town sprang up.

SALLY: That was a whole other time.

LORRAINE: Time's got nothin' to do with it.

SALLY: I'm stayin'.

(Pause)

LORRAINE: (Moves to JAKE) Jake, look—we were doin' just fine, weren't we? We had everything workin' smooth as butter here. We had our system. We were self-sufficient, weren't we, Jake? What do we need her for?

JAKE: I can trust her.

(Pause)

LORRAINE: *(Laughs)* I have been doin' my best to pull you out of this thing. I went outa my way to bring you back here. I fixed up your room, just like it used to be. I've been cookin' all your meals.

JAKE: It's just a trap.

LORRAINE: For what? Why would I wanna trap you? Have you got your mind so twisted up that you can't even recognize your own mother's good intentions?

JAKE: *(About* SALLY*)* I recognize *her.* I remember her real good. We went through somethin' together.

*(*JAKE *fixes on* SALLY *as he speaks about her.* SALLY*'s back is toward stage left. Very slowly, as this scene continues, light begins to rise on the stage-left set. A soft pool of light on the sofa where* FRANKIE *lies on his back with his head Upstage.* BETH *is kneeling on the floor next to* FRANKIE*, wrapping the shirt she wore in the first scene around* FRANKIE*'s wounded leg. Her gestures are very soft and loving. She wears jeans and a bra.* FRANKIE *is sweating hard and his face is extremely pale, like* JAKE*'s now.* JAKE *slowly approaches* SALLY *as he speaks to her.* SALLY, LORRAINE *and* JAKE *pay no attention to the stage-left light.)*

LORRAINE: Well, so did we, Jake. I've known you a lot longer than she has.

JAKE: *(Approaching* SALLY *slowly)* Where was that, Sally? Where was that? Where were we when that happened?

SALLY: You don't wanna know.

JAKE: We drove all night long.

SALLY: Just forget about it now.

(SALLY *moves away from* JAKE, *crosses to bed and sits on it.* JAKE *stays where he is, facing stage left. Now he begins to see* BETH *and* FRANKIE *in the dim light but he regards them as a distant vision in his mind.* LORRAINE *and* SALLY *ignore the stage-left action.* JAKE *remains fixed on* BETH *and* FRANKIE.)

JAKE: *(Staring at* BETH *and* FRANKIE) We listened to the radio.

(LORRAINE *crosses to* SALLY *carrying the tray of dirty plates.*)

LORRAINE: *(To* SALLY) See the state you've got him in now. See what you've done.

SALLY: *(Sitting on bed)* I haven't done a thing but come back home.

(SALLY *reaches under the bed and pulls out the flag. She spreads it across her lap.*)

LORRAINE: *(To* SALLY) You did it on purpose. You knew this was gonna happen. He was doin' so well with me lookin' after him. He was gonna stay. He was just gonna live here like he used to. Now you've got his mind all driftin' away again.

JAKE: *(Still fixed on* BETH *and* FRANKIE) We drove a thousand miles and never said a word.

LORRAINE: *(After pause, to* SALLY) Well, you stay then. You suit yourself. I'll just wait you out. I can wait a whole lot longer than you can. Believe you me. I've been a lifetime at it. He'll come back around to me. You wait and see. He'll come back.

(LORRAINE *exits upstage with tray and plates.* JAKE *stays fixed on* BETH *and* FRANKIE. SALLY *stares at* JAKE's *back. Pause.*)

JAKE: *(With his back to* SALLY) You gotta help me escape, Sally. I gotta get back there. She's still alive.

(SALLY *watches* JAKE *awhile, then reaches down under bed and pulls out the leather box of ashes. She holds it in her lap and opens it as* JAKE *remains staring stage left.*)

SALLY: What's this?

(JAKE *slowly turns around facing* SALLY. *They stare at each other as lights fade on them to black. Lights are rising on* BETH *and* FRANKIE *simultaneously.)*

SCENE 3

Lights remain up on stage-left set with FRANKIE *on his back stretched out on sofa, head upstage, and* BETH *on her knees beside him, wrapping* BAYLOR'S *shirt around his injured leg.*

FRANKIE: Uh—look—Beth—don't you think you oughta put your shirt back on?

BETH: You need it.

FRANKIE: I don't. Really. I don't. It's stopped bleeding. It hasn't bled for a long time now.

BETH: It could start again.

FRANKIE: It just aches a little. It's not bleeding anymore.

BETH: It's going up your leg now.

FRANKIE: *(Sits up fast)* What is?

BETH: Black line. That's bad.

FRANKIE: What's that mean? A black line.

*(*FRANKIE *pulls his pant leg up. Looks at his leg.)*

BETH: It's bad. Poison.

FRANKIE: *(Pushing his pant leg down again)* Look—please, just leave it alone and put your shirt back on. Your dad might come back in here.

71

BETH: He's asleep.

FRANKIE: Well, then your mother or your brother could come. Somebody could come in here.

BETH: Doesn't matter.

FRANKIE: It does matter! I'm on thin ground as it is without them seeing you on your knees with your shirt off. What're they gonna think if they walk in here and find you rubbing my leg with no shirt on? Please stop rubbing my leg now!

BETH: Don't you like it?

FRANKIE: Just stand up. Stand up on your feet and put your shirt back on. Please, Beth. Just act like we're having a conversation or something.

BETH: You don't have to be afraid of them. They're afraid of you.

FRANKIE: How do you figure that?

BETH: They tell it in their voice.

FRANKIE: They want to kill me.

BETH: Only Mike. But he won't.

FRANKIE: What makes you so sure about that?

BETH: *(Quick)* Because only half of him believes you're what he hates. The other half knows it's not true.

(Pause. FRANKIE stares at her.)

FRANKIE: I thought you couldn't uh—

BETH: What?

FRANKIE: *(Lies back down)* I don't know. I thought you couldn't talk right or something. You sound okay to me.

BETH: I do?

FRANKIE: Yeah. Your dad said there was—I mean you were having some kind of trouble.

BETH: Oh. There was that time. I don't know. I get them mixed. I get the thought. Mixed. It dangles. Sometimes the thought just hangs with no words there.

FRANKIE: But you can speak all right?

BETH: It speaks. Speeches. Speaking. In me. Comes and goes. Again. I don't know why. You hear me? Now?

FRANKIE: Yes. You sound all right. I mean it sounds like you're doing pretty good.

BETH: Sounds like it.

FRANKIE: Yeah.

BETH: You can speak? Speech.

FRANKIE: Me, Yeah, sure.

BETH: But you can't walk.

FRANKIE: No. Not right now.

BETH: I would rather walk than talk.

FRANKIE: Yeah—do you—would you mind getting up off the floor, please, and putting your shirt back on?

BETH: Maybe they'll have to cut your leg off.

FRANKIE: *(Sits up fast again)* What? Who do you mean?

BETH: Maybe cut. Like me. Cut me. Cut you out. Like me. See?

(She bends her head forward and pulls the hair up on the back of her neck to show FRANKIE *a nonexistent scar.* FRANKIE *looks at the place on her head that she's showing him.)*

BETH: *(Showing* FRANKIE *back of her head)* See? Tracks. Knife tracks.

FRANKIE: *(Looking at her head)* What? There's nothing there. There's no scar there.

BETH: *(Straightens her head again)* No brain. Cut me out. Cut. Brain. Cut.

FRANKIE: No, Beth, look—they didn't—they didn't operate did they? Nobody said anything about that.

BETH: They don't say. Secret. Like my old Mom. Old. My Grand Mom. Old. They cut her. Out. Disappeared. They don't say her name now. She's gone. Vanish. *(She makes a "whooshing" sound like wind.)* My Father sent her someplace. Had her gone.

FRANKIE: They wouldn't just go in there and operate without your consent. They can't do that. It's a law. They need written consent or something. Somebody has to sign something.

BETH: Mike.

FRANKIE: What?

BETH: Mike did.

FRANKIE: No, Beth. I don't think you've got this right. Mike wouldn't do something like that.

BETH: He wants me out.

FRANKIE: He's your brother. He loves you.

BETH: *(Stands, moves away from FRANKIE)* You don't know him!

FRANKIE: Well, there's no scar there, Beth. *(Unwraps the shirt from his leg and offers it out to her.)* Here, take this shirt back. Please. Come and take it.

(Pause. Slowly BETH bends down and takes shirt. She stands with it and holds it out away from herself. She giggles to herself.)

BETH: *(Holding shirt out)* Look how big a man is. So big. He scares himself. His shirt scares him. He puts his scary shirt on so it won't scare himself. He can't see it when it's on him. Now he thinks it's him.

(She giggles and puts the shirt back on. Buttons it up. FRANKIE watches her, still sitting on sofa.)

Jake was scared of shirts. You too?

FRANKIE: No. I'm only scared of people.

(BETH starts moving in circles, pulling the front of the shirt out away from herself and looking at the buttons and fabric.)

BETH: *(Referring to shirt)* This is like a custom. Big. Too big. Like a custom.

FRANKIE: A what?

BETH: Custom. Like a custom.

FRANKIE: A custom?

BETH: For play. Acting.

FRANKIE: Oh. You mean a "costume"?

BETH: Costume.

FRANKIE: Yeah. A "costume." I get what you mean.

BETH: Pretend.

FRANKIE: You were in a play, right? I mean you were acting.

BETH: *(Moving, playing with shirt)* Pretend is more better.

FRANKIE: What do you mean?

BETH: Pretend. Because it fills me. Pretending fills. Not empty. Other. Ordinary. Is no good. Empty. Ordinary is empty. Now, I'm like the man. *(Pumps her chest up, closes her fists, sticks her chin out and struts in the shirt.)* Just feel like the man. Shirt brings me a man. I am a shirt man. Can you see? Like father. You see me? Like brother. *(She laughs.)*

FRANKIE: Yeah. You liked acting, huh?

(BETH *keeps moving, finding variations of the shirt to play with.* FRANKIE *sits on sofa watching her.)*

BETH: Pretend to be. Like you. Between us we can make a life. You could be the woman. You be.

FRANKIE: What was the play you were in? Do you remember?

BETH: *(Moving toward* FRANKIE*)* You could pretend to be in love with me. With my shirt. You love my shirt. This shirt is a man to you. You are my beautiful woman. You lie down.

(BETH *moves in to* FRANKIE *and tries to push him down on the sofa by the shoulders.* FRANKIE *resists.*)

FRANKIE: Now, wait a second, Beth. Wait, wait. Come on.

(BETH *keeps trying to push* FRANKIE *back down on sofa but* FRANKIE *stays sitting.*)

BETH: *(Giggling, pushing* FRANKIE*)* You fight but all the time you want my smell. You want my shirt in your mouth. You dream of it. Always. You want me on your face.

(FRANKIE *pushes her away hard, then sits on edge of sofa.* BETH *stands away from him.*)

FRANKIE: *(Pushing her away)* Now cut it out!

(*Pause as* BETH *stares at him from a distance.*)

Now, look—I can't hang around here. I didn't come here to fool around. I've gotta get back home and talk to Jake about this. That's the whole reason I came here. He's gonna think something went wrong.

BETH: Jake.

FRANKIE: Yeah, He's gonna think somethin' happened to me.

BETH: Your other one. You have his same voice. Maybe you could be him. Pretend. Maybe. Just him. Just like him. But soft. With me. Gentle. Like a woman-man.

(BETH *starts moving slowly toward* FRANKIE. FRANKIE *stands awkwardly, supporting himself by the sofa, on his bad leg.*)

FRANKIE: I need to find some transportation outa here! I need to find my car! I can't hang around here, Beth.

BETH: *(Moving toward* FRANKIE*)* You could be better. Better man. Maybe. Without hate. You could be my sweet man. You could. Pretend to be. Try. My sweetest man.

(As BETH *gets closer,* FRANKIE *starts to move around the sofa, hopping on his bad leg and trying to keep the sofa between him and* BETH.*)*

FRANKIE: *(Hopping away from her)* No, Beth. This is not something I want to do right now. It's not good for my leg. I should be resting it. I have to be getting out of here now.

BETH: *(Moving after him slowly)* You could pretend so much that you start thinking this is me. You could really fall in love with me. How would that be? In a love we never knew.

FRANKIE: You're Jake's wife. We've got no business messing around like this! Now it's time for me to go. I have to go now. I have to find my car.

BETH: It's buried.

FRANKIE: What?

BETH: There's a blizzard. It's buried. We have to stay together now. Us. That's funny how we wind up. *(Laughs.)*

FRANKIE: A blizzard? What're you talking about, a blizzard. How long was I asleep?

BETH: *(Moving toward porch, pointing out)* See? Look. Out there. Everything's white.

FRANKIE: *(Trying to move away from sofa, toward porch)* When did that happen?

BETH: We have to stay alone. Together. Here. Us.

*(*FRANKIE *takes a couple of hopping steps and falls to the floor.* BETH *moves to him.)*

FRANKIE: *(On floor)* Goddamnit!

*(*FRANKIE *clutches his leg in pain.* BETH *kneels beside him and starts to take her shirt off again.* FRANKIE *stops her, reaches out and grabs her wrists.)*

No! Look—don't take your shirt off again! Don't do it. The shirt is not gonna do my leg any good. It's useless. Understand? The shirt is no help. So just leave it on. Okay? Just leave the shirt on, Beth.

(He lets go of her wrists. She stops trying to take the shirt off.)

BETH: Maybe they'll cut. Cut.

FRANKIE: Stop saying that! I don't like the sound of it. It's not as bad as all that. Amputation is not the answer here. Is there any way you could make a phone call for me?

(BETH stands, moves to sofa and sits. She watches FRANKIE on the floor.)

BETH: *(Sitting on sofa)* You can only think of far away? Only thoughts of where you came from? Nothing here? Nothing right here? Now.

FRANKIE: I'm in a situation here that I didn't expect to be in. You understand me? I didn't expect to be stuck here.

BETH: Stuck. Like me. Stuck.

FRANKIE: This is your home. You live here. I don't.

BETH: But you have brain.

FRANKIE: What?

BETH: Brain. In you. Thinking.

FRANKIE: So do you!

BETH: No. Mike took it. My father told him to.

(She gets up from sofa and crosses past FRANKIE to porch. She looks out. FRANKIE on floor behind her.)

FRANKIE: Beth, that's just not true. That's not true. I don't know where you got that idea from. You'd be dead if you didn't have a brain. You can't live without one.

BETH: *(Looking out over porch)* Then why is this so empty? So empty now. Everything. Gone. A hole.

(Sounds of MIKE *breathing heavily offstage.)*

FRANKIE: What's that? Beth? What's that sound? Is someone out there? Beth.

*(*BETH *continues looking out over porch.)*

Help me get back on the couch now. There's somebody coming.

*(*MIKE *enters from the porch, covered in snow and carrying the severed hindquarters of a large buck with the hide still on it. He carries the butchered deer over his right shoulder with his rifle in his left hand.* MIKE *sees* FRANKIE *on the floor. He stops. Pause. He stares at* BETH, *then back to* FRANKIE. MIKE *flops the hindquarters down on the floor in the middle of the room, then props his rifle on top of the meat. He pulls his gloves off and starts warming his hands by blowing into them.* FRANKIE *stares at* MIKE *from the floor.* BETH *stares at the deer parts. Pause.)*

MIKE: *(To* BETH, *but staring at* FRANKIE) Tell Dad I kept the rack for myself. It's a trophy buck. He can have the meat but I'm keepin' the rack.

BETH: *(Still staring at deer)* He doesn't eat the meat. Momma says he doesn't eat the meat.

MIKE: Then he can feed it to the dog. I don't care what he does with it. *(Pause. To* FRANKIE) What're you doin' on the floor?

FRANKIE: I can't get up.

MIKE: *(To* BETH) He didn't try nothin', did he?

(Pause. BETH *keeps staring at the deer.)*

Beth!

BETH: Huh?

MIKE: He didn't try to pull anything on ya, did he?

FRANKIE: I fell.

MIKE: *(To* FRANKIE*)* I'm askin' her!

BETH: *(Staring at deer)* You cut him in half?

MIKE: Beth, I'm askin' you a question!

*(*MEG *enters from up left in nightgown and bathrobe, slippers. She just appears, drowsy from sleep.)*

MEG: Why is there so much noise now? Your father's trying to get some sleep.

MIKE: He should try sleepin' at night like everybody else.

FRANKIE: *(To* MEG*)* Mam—

MEG: *(To* FRANKIE*)* Why aren't you up on the sofa? You're gonna catch your death of cold on the floor like that.

BETH: Mama? Daddy doesn't eat the meat, does he?

*(*MEG *looks at* BETH, *then she sees the deer carcass on the floor. She approaches it slowly, stepping over* FRANKIE.*)*

Mike said to give it to Daddy but he doesn't eat the meat.

MEG: *(Staring at deer quarters)* Mike—what in the world? Can't you take it down to the freezer?

MIKE: Tell Dad to do it when he gets up. I shot it for him, he can dress it out. I'm goin' back out there. There's deer all over the place.

MEG: Well, you can't just leave it here in the middle of the living room floor.

MIKE: Why not? It's frozen solid. Won't thaw out for hours yet. I thought I'd surprise him.

MEG: He'll be surprised all right.

FRANKIE: *(Still on floor, trying to crawl to sofa)* Mam, is there any chance you could make a phone call for me?

MEG: I suppose so. Is it long distance?

MIKE: Nobody's makin' any phone calls for you, buddy. The lines are frozen solid. You're stuck. You're stuck right here. It's snowin' like there's no tomorrow out there.

MEG: *(Moving toward porch, looking out)* Is it that bad? I must've dozed off. It wasn't snowing that hard when I went upstairs.

FRANKIE: *(Reaching sofa, trying to pull himself up)* I have to get back home! I can't stay here anymore! I have to get back home!

MEG: *(Staring out over porch at snow)* Please, don't scream in the house. This house is very old.

FRANKIE: *(Clawing his way up onto sofa, to MIKE)* Look—look—you want me outa here, right? Everybody wants me outa here? I don't belong here, right? I'm not part of your family. I'm an enemy to you? Isn't that right? I am willing to go. Now. I'm ready. I'm ready to go now! Just get me outa here whatever way you can. I'll do whatever's necessary. I'll pay you. Just get me outa here!

(MIKE smiles and stares at FRANKIE, puts his gloves back on, picks up his rifle. BETH crosses slowly over to FRANKIE. FRANKIE collapses, exhausted, on sofa.)

BETH: *(Beside FRANKIE now, she pats him softly on his head)* Your whole life can turn around. Upside down. In a flash. Sudden. Don't worry. Don't worry now. This whole world can disappear. Everything you know can go. You won't even recognize your own hands.

(BETH, as she exits, moves slowly upstage and exits through hallway entrance.)

Night, Mama.

MEG: Good night, dear.

MIKE: *(To* MEG*)* It's not night! It's daytime! Jesus Christ, can't you see it's daytime out there.

*(*MEG *turns slowly and stares out over porch.* MIKE *exits out porch, down stairs and disappears upstage with his rifle.* MEG *stays looking out over porch.)*

FRANKIE: *(Yelling to* MIKE *as he exits)* Wait a second!

(Pause. FRANKIE *and* MEG *are left alone,* MEG, *with her back to* FRANKIE, *staring out at snow.* FRANKIE *stares at her back.)*

MEG: *(Keeping her back to* FRANKIE, *staring out)* I never get tired of seeing snow. Isn't that funny?

(Lights fade to black.)

SCENE 4

Lights up on stage-right set. Night. Moon is full. SALLY *is in* JAKE's *bed with the blanket pulled up around her neck, lying on her back.* JAKE *is standing in the middle of the room in his underwear still, leather jacket with medals. He's draping the flag around his neck and over his shoulders, holding the leather box of ashes in one hand.*

SALLY: This isn't gonna fool her, Jake.

JAKE: *(Moving to bed)* Just tuck yourself in. Tuck the blanket tight around you so she sees there's a body in there.

(He goes to SALLY *and starts tucking the blanket tightly around her with her arms inside and only her head sticking out.)*

SALLY: But my body doesn't look anything like your body.

JAKE: Doesn't matter. She's not gonna look that close. Turn over on your stomach so she doesn't see your face.

SALLY: She'll see my hair then.

JAKE: Put your head under the pillow. Turn over and put your head under the pillow. Come on, Sally. You gotta do it.

*(*SALLY *turns herself over on her stomach as* JAKE *keeps tucking the blanket around her tightly.)*

SALLY: This is really stupid, Jake. Where'd you see this, in some old prison movie?

JAKE: *(Tucking blanket around her, then putting pillow over her head)* Now when she comes in, in the morning—she'll come in with the breakfast. She'll come in and she'll say somethin' like: "Rise and shine—it's coffee time!" You just stay under the pillow. You can kinda moan or somethin'—make a few little movements, but don't say anything to her.

(SALLY takes the pillow off her head and throws it on floor.)

SALLY: *(Throwing pillow)* I can't breathe under here! I feel like a mummy.

(JAKE picks up pillow.)

JAKE: Sally, you gotta cover your head or she'll know right away.

SALLY: All right, just hand me the pillow. When I hear her comin', I'll put it over my head.

JAKE: What if you fall asleep? You could fall asleep and forget.

SALLY: I won't forget. Just hand me the pillow.

(Pause. JAKE tosses the pillow on her head. SALLY takes it and moves it to one side. Pause.)

You better go through the bathroom window. She'll see you if you try to cross the porch.

JAKE: I know how to escape. Don't worry.

SALLY: Aren't you gonna wear any pants?

JAKE: She hid 'em. She thinks that's gonna stop me.

SALLY: You're gonna try to get to Montana in your underpants with an American flag wrapped around your neck?

JAKE: I'll travel by night.

SALLY: *(Laughs)* Oh boy, Jake. I hope ya make it.

JAKE: I'll make it all right. There's nothin' gonna stop me. Not Frankie or Mom or that family of hers or—

(He stops himself. Stares into space.)

SALLY: What'sa matter, Jake?

JAKE: *(Staring)* There's this thing—this thing in my head.

(SALLY rises up slowly on one elbow in the bed and stares at him. He whispers now.)

(Whisper) This thing that the next moment—the moment right after this one will—blow up. Explode with a voice. A scream from a voice I don't know. Or a voice I knew once but now it's changed. It doesn't know me either. Now. It used to but not now. I've scared it into something else. Another form. A whole other person who doesn't see me anymore. Who doesn't even remember that we knew each other once. I've gotta see her again, Sally.

(Suddenly BETH screams from out of the darkness, stage left.)

BETH: *(In dark)* JAAAAAAAAAAAAAAKE!

(Lights black out stage right.)

Act III

SCENE 1

Stage-right set. LORRAINE *is in* JAKE*'s bed bundled up in blankets to her neck. She shakes all over with the cold chills and her face is pale and sweating. The model airplanes still hang overhead.* SALLY *sits in the chair, stage left of the bed, with a bowl of soup on her lap and a spoon in her hand. A cup of coffee sits steaming on the side table.* SALLY*'s voice is heard first in darkness.*

SALLY: *(In dark)* Rise and shine! It's coffee time!

> *(Lights sweep up fast to bright morning.* SALLY *offers* LORRAINE *a spoonful of soup.)*

LORRAINE: Did he tell you to say that? He probably did, didn't he? Where is the humiliation supposed to end?

SALLY: Just try a little sip of soup, Mom. Just a little sip.

LORRAINE: Not from you.

SALLY: Look, you can't keep blaming me forever. He's gone. There was nothin' I could do about it.

LORRAINE: Is there any good reason in this Christless world why men leave women? Is there? Is there any good reason for that? You tell me. You tell me. Isn't there enough to suffer already? We got all kinda good reasons to suffer without men cookin' up more.

SALLY: There's always a chance he might come back.

LORRAINE: He won't come back now. Thanks to you. Not now. I know him. He's like a stray dog. He's home for a while and you pet him and feed him and he licks your hand and then he's gone again. I know where he's gone too. Straight to that girl. You can bet yer bivey on that. She's got a hold on his mind.

SALLY: Well, Frankie'll bring him back then. He'll find him.

LORRAINE: Frankie can't even find his own zipper. How's he gonna find his brother?

SALLY: Just try a little soup, Mom.

LORRAINE: I don't want any a' that slop! Stop tryin' to pawn it off on me.

SALLY: It's the same batch you made for Jake.

LORRAINE: I know. Smells like it.

SALLY: (Smelling soup) Smells all right to me.

LORRAINE: It's ripe.

SALLY: Well, you gotta eat somethin'.

LORRAINE: My son's abandoned me! Can't you understand that? He's abandoned me. And you put him up to it.

SALLY: I didn't put him up to nothin'. What was he gonna do? Stay here and rot in this room. He woulda left sooner or later.

LORRAINE: He's run off to the wild world when he could've stayed here under my protection. He could've stayed here forever and no one could've touched him. Now he's gonna wind up right back in prison. In prison, where they'll eat him alive.

SALLY: (Offering spoon to LORRAINE) Just take a little bit on your tongue. See if you like it.

(LORRAINE sits up fast and knocks the spoon out of SALLY's hand. SALLY stands and moves left, away from LORRAINE.)

LORRAINE: (As she knocks spoon away) Get that stuff away from me! What'sa matter with you! I'm not interested in food. I'm not interested in keeping something alive that's already dead.

SALLY: You're not dead yet! You won't get out of it that easy!

(Pause)

LORRAINE: I know what's gonna happen. I can see it plain as day. They'll find him by the highway. That's what'll happen. Crumpled up. Busted open like a road dog. Then maybe you'll be satisfied.

SALLY: I don't want anything to happen to him any more than you do. He couldn't stay here.

LORRAINE: I'll get a call. Cop will come to my door. Just like before. Just like with his daddy. I'll wait for that cop. I'll wait right here. Long as I have to.

SALLY: Now don't start imagining things.

LORRAINE: There's nothin' imaginary about it. I can see it.

SALLY: What can you see?

LORRAINE: Maybe the same cop will come. The very same cop. I never could figure that out. Why they'd send a cop? Why should a cop be a messenger of death? It's like sending a fireman.

(LORRAINE lies back down in bed again. She pulls the blankets up around her neck. Pause.)

SALLY: You can't let yourself get so worked up over this. You're gonna make yourself sick.

LORRAINE: You sent that cop, didn't you? Back then. Jake never woulda done somethin' like that. He'da come and told me face to face.

SALLY: We were miles away. Mexico. It happened in Mexico. Remember?

LORRAINE: I remember! Don't talk to me like I'm an idiot.

SALLY: We tried to call you that night it happened. We both tried to call you but they said the police had to do it. It was international. I never wanted to send a cop. They said it had to be official.

LORRAINE: Doesn't matter. Official, unofficial, it's the same news. Dead is dead. Nobody can make it un-dead.

(Pause)

SALLY: You didn't really care one way or the other, did you? You'd let him go a long time ago.

LORRAINE: He left me! All right? Get that straight in your noggin. *He* left *me!* Not the other way around.

SALLY: You never tried to find him.

LORRAINE: *(Sitting up again)* Are you kidding? Man runs off. Into the night. No word. No note. No phone call. Disappears like an apparition and I'm supposed to go track his ass down. Not me, sister. No sir. Not this one. Let him stagger around, lost and wild-eyed if he wants to. Let him bang his head up and down the alleyways moanin' like a baby about some mystery he doesn't even have a clue to. You can't save the doomed! You make a stab at it. You make the slightest little try and you're doomed yourself. Take a look at your brother if you don't believe me.

SALLY: But you never even tried, did you?

LORRAINE: Tried what? Who are you to be judgin' me now? Who are you? You don't even have a man. Never did.

SALLY: You're not recommending it, are you?

LORRAINE: Just don't go accusing me of neglecting your father. You don't know nothin' about it.

SALLY: You never even asked me about it.

LORRAINE: About what?

SALLY: Our trip down there. Me and Jake made a special trip. Remember? We found him in his trailer down there.

LORRAINE: *(Lies back down)* So what? Ya want a medal or somethin'? You're his kids, not his wife. Why shouldn't you try to find him. I don't wanna hear about that stuff now.

SALLY: We really surprised him. I don't think he'd had a visitor for months.

LORRAINE: Who'd visit him?

SALLY: He didn't even know who we were at first. Just stood there at the screen door, kinda staring at us like we might be burglars or something.

LORRAINE: Probably drunk. As usual.

SALLY: Nope. Stone cold sober. Didn't have any money to drink. He looked real weak and vulnerable. The opposite of how he was when he was drinking.

LORRAINE: He was always weak. That never changed.

SALLY: He took us inside and the smell almost knocked me over. No windows. Smelled like dirty laundry and cigarettes and something else. Something almost sweet.

LORRAINE: Booze.

SALLY: Maybe.

LORRAINE: Tiger Rose. That was his baby. Tiger Rose. I musta tripped over a million a' them skinny green bottles.

SALLY: He had all these pictures of us taped to the walls. Baby pictures and 4-H Club pictures and pictures of Jake running with a football. But they were all squeezed in between these other pictures. Pictures of Bing Crosby and Ginger Rogers and Ida Lupino and Gene Autry and Louis Armstrong. And there we were kinda peeking out between the cracks of these faces. I got the feeling he must've spent a lot of time talking to these faces. Maybe even introducing the pictures of us to the pictures of all these stars. Trying to make a family out of us all. So we'd know each other.

LORRAINE: Yeah, well he shoulda tried that at home first.

SALLY: You can't condemn him now. He's dead.

LORRAINE: I'll condemn him right up to my last breath! He shaped my whole life. Vengeance is the only thing that keeps me goin'.

SALLY: How can you get revenge out of a dead man?

LORRAINE: Because—he's still alive in me. You understand that? He's still walkin' around inside me. He put stuff into me that'll never go away. Ever. He made sure a' that.

SALLY: That's not him. That's you. If you hadn't had him, you'da found somebody else to throw the blame on.

LORRAINE: Yeah, well you didn't know him like I knew him.

SALLY: Guess not. Because what I saw down there with Jake was a man who was totally innocent.

LORRAINE: Innocent! That's a hot one.

SALLY: Didn't you ever wonder about him? About what became of him?

LORRAINE: Who?

SALLY: Dad.

LORRAINE: (Sitting up) Wonder? Did I ever wonder? You know a man your whole life. You grow up with him. You're almost raised together. You go to school on the same bus together. You go through tornadoes together in the same basement. You go through a world war together. You have babies together. And then one day he just up and disappears into thin air. Did I ever wonder? Yeah. You bet your sweet life I wondered. But you know where all that wondering got me? Nowhere. Absolutely nowhere. Because here I am. Here I am. Alone. Just the same as though he'd never even existed.

SALLY: I thought you said he was still in you.

LORRAINE: Not him. Some disease he left behind.

SALLY: But there must've been a time when you loved him. Before.

LORRAINE: Love. Whata crock a' shit. Love! There's another disease. Only difference is it's a disease that makes ya feel good. While it lasts. Then, when it's gone, yer worse off than before you caught it.

SALLY: Well, I don't think there's a whole lot we can do about it, is there?

LORRAINE: Yes there is. Oh, yes there is. You can resist. You can look it right square in the kisser and resist.

(LORRAINE lies back down. Pause.)

SALLY: Maybe. Maybe *you* can. That's what Jake tried to do. He's a lot like you I guess. He started squirming in that trailer. Making up reasons why we had to get outa there. Get back across the border before it got dark. Dad kept wanting us to stay but he didn't have anything to offer us. And that's when Jake made a desperate move. He didn't even know he was doing it. He was so desperate to get out of that situation, that he stands up and he offers to take Dad and me out to a bar. For a drink! I couldn't believe it. Dad's whole face lit up. I've never seen his face like that. He smiled like a little kid and grabbed his hat.

LORRAINE: You can't stop a drinkin' man from drinkin'. All he needs is an idea and he's gone. Just the idea of straddling a bar stool in some honky-tonk somewhere in his mind. He's gone.

(LORRAINE slowly pulls herself up to a sitting position and listens more intently to SALLY.)

SALLY: They started right off with double shots of tequila and lime. At first it was like this brotherhood they'd just remembered. But then it started to shift. After about the fourth double shot it started to go in a whole different direction.

LORRAINE: That figures.

SALLY: There was a meanness that started to come outa both of them like these hidden snakes. A terrible meanness that was like— murder almost. It *was* murder.

LORRAINE: Whad'ya mean, murder?

SALLY: Their eyes changed. Something in their eyes. Like animals. Like the way an animal looks for the weakness in another animal. They started poking at each other's weakness. Stabbing. Just a little bit at a time. Like the way that rooster used to do. That rooster we had that went around looking for the tiniest speck of blood on a hen or a chick and then he'd start pecking away at it. And the more he pecked at it the more excited he got until finally he just killed it.

LORRAINE: Yeah, we had to boil that one. Tough son of a gun.

SALLY: They locked into each other like there was nobody else in the bar. At first it was all about sports. About which one of them could throw a hardball faster. Which one could take the toughest hit in football. Which one could run the fastest and the longest. That was the one they decided would be the big test. They decided to prove it to each other once and for all. So they downed a couple more tequilas and crashed out through the doors of the place into the street.

LORRAINE: I thought you said he could barely stand up.

SALLY: Who?

LORRAINE: Your father.

SALLY: That was before. Before he'd had a drink. Now it was like he'd had a transfusion or somethin'. That tequila went right into his blood and lit him on fire. He crouched down in a racing position right beside Jake. And they were both deadly serious. And then they took off. Dad took about four strides and fell flat on his face in the street but Jake never stopped. He ran like a wild colt and never once looked back. Straight into the next bar up the block. I went over and tried to help Dad up but he turned on me and snarled. Just like a dog. Just exactly like a crazy dog. I saw it in his eyes. This deep, deep hate that came from somewhere far away. It was pure, black hate with no purpose.

LORRAINE: That was him all right.

SALLY: He wouldn't let me help him. He just crawled up the street toward the bar that Jake went into. And there I was following along behind. I felt so stupid. He kept turning and snarling at me to keep back. But I didn't wanna fall too far back 'cause I was afraid somethin'—

(She starts to break down but stops herself.)

LORRAINE: What?

SALLY: *(Trying to control it)* I was afraid somethin' bad might happen to him and—it happened anyway.

LORRAINE: What happened?

SALLY: Jake came up with a brilliant idea. He said, since we were only about a mile from the American border we should hit every bar and continue the race until we got to the other side. First one to the other side, won. First one to America! But we couldn't miss a bar. Right then I knew what Jake had in mind.

LORRAINE: What?

SALLY: Jake had decided to kill him.

(Pause)

LORRAINE: *(Throws the blankets off and struggles to sit up)* What in the world are you talkin' about!

SALLY: It was just the same—it was just the same as if he'd had a gun. He knew what was gonna happen. Dad couldn't even walk anymore. He couldn't stand. His knees were all bloody. Jake knew that all he had to do was push him over the edge. Just a few more drinks and he'd be gone.

LORRAINE: *(Struggling to stand by bed, supporting herself)* That is the most lamebrained, idiotic piece of claptrap I ever heard in my life! Jake might be a lot a' things. He might be crazy. He might be wound a little loose in some areas but he would never, ever, in this world, try to kill his own father! How can you say somethin' like that?

SALLY: I was there! I was right there and I saw every inch of it. I saw him killed! I saw it happen. I saw him splattered all over the road like some lost piece of livestock. He was trying to run down the middle of a highway. He was trying to beat his own son to the border. He didn't even know what country he was in anymore! Jake murdered him! And he never even looked back. He was already sitting in some bar down the road ordering the next round of drinks. He never even got up when he heard the sirens.

LORRAINE: It was an accident! That's all. Just an ordinary accident. Couldn't be helped.

SALLY: No, Mom. It was no accident.

LORRAINE: He didn't know what he was doin', any more than his father did!

SALLY: He knew. He still knows. He made me promise. That's how come he didn't tell you face to face. That's why the cop came to your door.

LORRAINE: He is not a murderer! My son is not a murderer! Why is everyone trying to make him into this criminal? First, that woman of his. He never shoulda got tied up with that woman in the first place. She's the cause of all this. And now you've turned against him.

SALLY: I'm just tellin' you what I saw with my own eyes.

LORRAINE: What you saw? What you saw! You stood there and watched your own father get run over by a truck in the middle of a Mexican highway and you're tryin' to tell me that Jake murdered him?

SALLY: That's the way it happened.

LORRAINE: What about you! Jake was nowhere near him you said. What were you doin'? Standin' there helpless? You were the only one sober and there was nothin' you could do? Is that the story?

SALLY: Dad wouldn't let me near him. I couldn't get near him.

LORRAINE: You couldn't have gone for help? Were your legs broke or somethin'?

SALLY: There was nowhere to go! Jake had the keys.

LORRAINE: Jake! Jake! Jake! *You're* the one who killed him, not Jake!! You're the one. If he was that drunk, you could've taken care of him. You coulda got him off the road. You coulda dragged him. You coulda done somethin' other than just stand there and watch. It was you. Wasn't it? It was you that wanted him dead. It's you that wants Jake dead too!

SALLY: No!

LORRAINE: It's you that wants to undermine this entire family! Drag us down one by one until there's no one left but you.

SALLY: I'm just sick of coverin' up for him. I'm sick to death of covering everything up. I'm sick of being locked up in this room. In our own house. Look at this room. What're we doin' in here? This was Jake's room when he was a kid. What're we doin' in this room now? What're we supposed to be hiding from?

(Long pause. LORRAINE *stands there staring at* SALLY, *then slowly turns her head up and stares at the model planes.)*

LORRAINE: *(Staring at planes)* I know one thing for sure. All these airplanes have gotta go. All these airplanes are comin' down. Every last one of 'em. All the junk in this house that they left behind for me to save. It's all goin'. We'll make us a big bonfire. They never wanted it anyway. They had no intention of ever comin' back here to pick it up. That was just a dream of theirs. It never meant a thing to them. They dreamed it up just to keep me on the hook. Can't believe I fell for it all those years.

SALLY: I didn't want him to die, Mom.

LORRAINE: Doesn't matter now. He was one a' them hopeless men. Nothin' you can do about the hopeless. *(Pause)* You know what I miss more than anything now?

SALLY: What?

LORRAINE: The wind. One a' them fierce, hot, dry winds that come from deep out in the desert and rip the trees apart. You know, those winds that wipe everything clean and leave the sky without a cloud. Pure blue. Pure, pure blue. Wouldn't that be nice?

(Lights fade slowly to black.)

SCENE 2

Lights up, stage-left set. Night. FRANKIE *asleep on couch, curled up, his back to audience with a dark blanket wrapped around him. Just as lights rise, we see* BAYLOR *drop himself heavily into the armchair, exhausted. He's wearing a gray long-john top, heavy dark woolen pants with suspenders (dark bloodstains on pants and shirt), heavy wool socks with the same boots from Act II but with the laces untied. He breathes heavily and makes a feeble attempt to lean forward and take his boots off but gives up and collapses back into the comfort of the chair, giving out a defeated exhale.* MEG *enters quickly from up left still in nightgown, bathrobe and slippers from Act II.*

MEG: Baylor, could you please come upstairs and talk to Beth? She's got me worried sick.

BAYLOR: Help me off with these boots, would ya? My back's killin' me. Some hunter. Leave all the work up to someone else. Easy enough to shoot the damn thing. Dressin' it out's another matter.

(MEG moves to BAYLOR, kneels and pulls his boots off. She stands again and keeps hold of the boots.)

MEG: *(Standing in front of him with boots)* Baylor.

BAYLOR: What! Stop houndin' me, will ya! "Baylor, Baylor, Baylor!" I never get a moment's peace around here.

MEG: I want you to come upstairs and talk to Beth.

BAYLOR: Tell her to come down here if she wants to talk. I'm not gettin' outa this chair for the duration of the night.

MEG: She won't come down.

BAYLOR: Then have her send me a letter. There's nothin' wrong with her body is there? Last time I saw her, she was walkin' around.

MEG: She's talking in a whole different way now. About stuff I never even heard of. I don't understand a thing. It's like she's talking to someone else.

BAYLOR: Well, she wasn't exactly an open book before.

MEG: I know, but now she's just scaring me really bad.

BAYLOR: Scarin' you? She's your own daughter for Christ's sake.

MEG: Well, she doesn't act like it anymore. She's like a whole different person.

BAYLOR: She's the same person. Just leave her be for a while. She needs some time to herself. Yer always fussin' with her so much she never has a chance to just be by herself. That's the only way she's gonna be able to face this thing.

MEG: I'm afraid to leave her alone, though.

BAYLOR: Stop bein' afraid! Yer afraid a' this—yer afraid a' that. You spend all yer time bein' afraid. Why don't ya just save all that fear up for when the real thing comes along.

MEG: What's that?

(Pause)

BAYLOR: Well, we're not gonna last forever, are we, Meg? Have ya ever given that any thought? One a' these days our parts are gonna give out on us and that'll be it. Now that's somethin' to be afraid of.

MEG: I'm not afraid a' that. I don't care one way or the other about that. I'm afraid for my daughter. She's disappearing on us. All I recognize anymore is her body. And even that's beginning to change.

BAYLOR: How do ya mean?

MEG: The way she stands now. With her shoulders all slumped forward and her head slung down. Her eyes staring at the ground all the time. She never used to be like that.

BAYLOR: She's had a big shock to her system. Whad'ya expect?

MEG: I expect her to get better. I expect her to come back to herself. She's a million miles away now.

BAYLOR: Well, we handled yer mother for all those years. We can handle Beth, too, I suppose.

MEG: My mother was an old, old woman. Beth's still a baby.

BAYLOR: She's not a baby.

MEG: She's a young woman! She's young yet, Baylor.

BAYLOR: I know she's young. What's that got to do with it? You think the powers that be hang around waiting for the right time, the right moment to bear down upon us? You think they're all sittin' up there consulting with each other about her age? "Oh, she's young yet. She's a baby. Let's hold off for a while." They couldn't give a shit about her predicament or any of us. We're all gonna get clobbered when we least expect it.

MEG: *(Moving to exit up left)* Well, I can't talk to you about it. That's clear.

BAYLOR: Where you goin'?

MEG: Upstairs.

BAYLOR: Bring me in that Mink Oil before you go up there. You think you can remember that? Last time you forgot. My feet are startin' to bleed.

(MEG exits up left through hallway with BAYLOR's boots. BAYLOR gives another deep exhale, then turns his head and stares at FRANKIE, who's still asleep. Pause. BAYLOR kicks the couch with his left foot, then flinches with pain, but FRANKIE remains asleep.)

BAYLOR: *(To* FRANKIE*)* Soon's the plow comes through, you're outa here, pal. This ain't a motel.

*(*BAYLOR *kicks the couch again and flinches but* FRANKIE *remains asleep.)*

You hear me?

*(*MEG *re-enters from the hallway with a tin of Mink Oil, crosses to* BAYLOR *and hands the tin to him.)*

(To MEG*)* We gotta get this character outa the house. He's dead weight. All he does is sleep now. *(To* MEG, *taking tin)* Thanks. Help me off with these socks, would ya? I can't bend an inch.

*(*MEG *kneels and pulls* BAYLOR*'s socks off while* BAYLOR *struggles to open the tin.)*

MEG: Beth's been talking about him. Saying his name. Did we know this man before, Dad?

BAYLOR: *(Slamming tin into the arm of the chair)* Goddamn these tins! They make everything nowadays so they won't come open! Nothin' comes open anymore.

MEG: Here, let me do it.

BAYLOR: *(Hands tin to* MEG*)* You do it.

MEG: *(Taking tin)* I am doing it.

*(*MEG *pops open the tin easily and hands it back to* BAYLOR.*)*

BAYLOR: How'd you do that?

MEG: I've done it before.

BAYLOR: Well, I can never get the damn thing to pop open. They used to have a little trigger on the side. Little metal pry gizmo.

MEG: They still do.

(BAYLOR turns the tin around until he discovers a little metal hinged bar.)

BAYLOR: I'll be darned. Thought they'd eliminated that.

MEG: No. They still have it.

BAYLOR: Well, I'll be darned. Would you mind puttin' this on my feet, Meg? My back is so sore from carving that meat, I can't bend over.

(BAYLOR hands the Mink Oil tin back to MEG. MEG takes it. She hesitates.)

MEG: I should get back upstairs and check on Beth.

BAYLOR: Just do my feet, would ya please!

(MEG kneels and starts to rub Mink Oil into BAYLOR's feet. BAYLOR lays his head back on the chair and closes his eyes.)

MEG: She's just been talking so funny. Mixing things up. I can't follow her thoughts anymore.

BAYLOR: Aah. Boy, I'm tellin' ya, that is as close to heaven as I been in a long time.

MEG: *(As she rubs his feet)* Doesn't it sting?

BAYLOR: Little bit.

MEG: I should think it would. Your toes are cracked wide open. How can you do that to yourself?

BAYLOR: I didn't do it. The cold did.

MEG: But you sit out there in that shack for hours on end letting your feet freeze. That doesn't make any sense, Baylor.

BAYLOR: I can't stalk deer anymore, at my age. I gotta wait for 'em to come to me.

MEG: Isn't there some other hobby you could take up?

BAYLOR: It's no hobby. Where'd you get that idea? Hunting is no hobby. It's an art. It's a way a' life. Everything gets turned into a hobby these days.

MEG: Well, it's not necessary to injure yourself like this.

BAYLOR: What's "necessary" got to do with it?

MEG: Well, I mean, we're living in the modern world. We've got the grocery store just four miles down the road. We don't need to kill animals anymore to stay alive. We're not pioneers.

BAYLOR: There's more to it than that.

MEG: Well, what is it? I'd like to know. I mean what is the big fascination about standing out there in the cold for hours on end waiting for an innocent deer to come along so you can blast a hole through it and freeze your feet off in the process?

BAYLOR: It's deer season. You hunt deer in deer season. That's what you do.

MEG: Look at this. You've got blood all over your pants and shirt. You look like you've been in a war or something.

BAYLOR: Just rub that stuff into my feet and stop tryin' to pick a bone with me. I'm too tired to argue.

(Pause. MEG *keeps rubbing* BAYLOR's feet. BAYLOR *keeps his eyes closed.*)

MEG: (After pause) Maybe you just wanna be alone. Maybe that's it. Maybe it's got nothing to do with hunting. You just don't want to be a part of us anymore.

BAYLOR: (Eyes closed) You've still got the greatest hands in the world.

MEG: Maybe it really is true that we're so different that we'll never be able to get certain things across to each other. Like mother used to say.

BAYLOR: Your mother.

MEG: "Two opposite animals."

BAYLOR: Your mother was a basket case.

MEG: She was a female.

(Pause. BAYLOR opens his eyes, looks at MEG, shakes his head, then closes his eyes again.)

BAYLOR: *(Eyes closed)* Meg, do you ever think about the things you say or do you just say 'em?

MEG: She was pure female. There wasn't any trace of male in her. Like Beth—Beth's got male in her. I can see that.

BAYLOR: I'm her father.

MEG: No. She's got male in her.

BAYLOR: *(Opens eyes, leans forward, points to himself)* I'm male! I'm her father and I'm a male! Now if you can't make sense, just don't speak. Okay? Just rub my feet and don't speak.

(BAYLOR leans back, closes his eyes again. MEG keeps on rubbing his feet. Pause.)

MEG: She was like a deer. Her eyes.

BAYLOR: Oh, brother. How do you manage to get things so screwed up? No wonder yer daughter's in the shape she's in. A deer is a deer and a person is a person. They got nothin' to do with each other.

(Pause)

MEG: Some people are like deer. They have that look—that distant thing in their eyes. Like mother did.

BAYLOR Your mother had that distant thing in her eyes because she'd lost her mind, Meg. She went crazy.

MEG: She was just old.

BAYLOR: Yeah, she almost took us to the grave with her. You and me'd be a lot younger today if we'd stuck her in a rest home when the whole thing started.

MEG: *(Still rubbing his feet)* I know what it is.

(Pause. BAYLOR *opens his eyes.)*

BAYLOR: What! What's what *what* is?

MEG: The female—the female one needs—the other.

BAYLOR: What other?

MEG: The male. The male one.

BAYLOR: Oh.

MEG: But the male one—doesn't really need the other. Not the same way.

BAYLOR: I don't get ya.

MEG: The male one goes off by himself. Leaves. He needs something else. But he doesn't know what it is. He doesn't really know what he needs. So he ends up dead. By himself.

*(*BAYLOR *sits up fast. Pulls his feet away from* MEG, *grabs the tin away from her and starts trying to put the lid back on it.)*

BAYLOR: All right. All right! Stop rubbing my feet now. Go on upstairs! Go on. I've heard enough a' this.

*(*MEG *stands.)*

MEG: Did I put enough on?

BAYLOR: Yeah, that's fine. Go on upstairs now.

MEG: You know, that stuff's not really for feet.

BAYLOR: What?

MEG: That Mink Oil. That's for boots. It's not made for feet.

BAYLOR: I know that! Don't ya think I don't know that!

MEG: I just thought maybe you didn't know that.

(BAYLOR starts reaching for his socks but can't quite get to them.)

BAYLOR: WILL YOU PLEASE GO ON UPSTAIRS NOW!!! GET
OUTA HERE!

*(Pause. MEG just stands there staring at him as BAYLOR trembles with
rage, trying to reach his socks.)*

MEG: You think it's me, don't you? You didn't used to think it was,
but now you think it's me. You think your whole life went sour
because of me. Because of Mother. Because of Beth. If only your
life was free of females, then you'd be free yourself.

BAYLOR: Well, you sure know how to speak the truth when you put yer
mind to it, don't ya?

MEG: All these women put a curse on you and now you're stuck.
You're chained to us forever. Isn't that the way it is?

BAYLOR: Yeah! Yeah! That's exactly the way it is. You got that right. I
could be up in the wild country huntin' antelope. I could be
raising a string a' pack mules back up in there. Doin' somethin'
useful. But no, I gotta play nursemaid to a bunch a' feeble-
minded women down here in civilization who can't take care a'
themselves. I gotta waste my days away makin' sure they eat
and have a roof over their heads and a nice warm place to go
crazy in.

MEG: Nobody's crazy, Baylor. Except you. Why don't you just go.
Why don't you just go off and live the way you want to live.
We'll take care of ourselves. We always have.

(MEG turns to go.)

BAYLOR: Wait a second!

(MEG stops, turns to him. Pause.)

Come and reach me my socks for me. I can't bend over.

(Pause. MEG *looks at socks, then to* BAYLOR.)

Just pick 'em up for me. You don't have to put 'em on me. I can do that by myself.

*(*MEG *crosses slowly over to his socks, picks them up off the floor, holds them up in the air. Pause.)*

Gimme my socks! My feet are freezing!

*(*MEG *moves slowly to* BAYLOR *with the socks and drops them in his lap, then turns and exits up left through hallway.* BAYLOR *struggles to put his socks on as he rages to himself but he can't get them on.)*

BAYLOR: *(To himself, struggling with socks)* Everything should be reversed! Everything should be reversed! The worst part of your life should come first, not last! Why do they save it for last when yer too old to do anything about it. When yer body's so tied up in knots you can't even stand up to yer own wife.

*(*BAYLOR *throws his socks down in defeat. He kicks the sofa and yells at* FRANKIE.)*

BAYLOR: *(To* FRANKIE) Hey! Hey! *(Kicks couch again.)* Hey, you goddamn freeloader! Nap time is over!

*(*FRANKIE *stays asleep.* BAYLOR *reaches out and pulls the blanket off him.)*

Get up! Get up outa that sofa before I drag you out of it with my own two hands!

*(*FRANKIE *stays asleep. Finally* BAYLOR *reaches out with his foot and pokes* FRANKIE *hard in the rear. Suddenly* FRANKIE *sits up, not knowing where he is. He grabs a corner of the blanket and tries to pull it back around himself but* BAYLOR *grabs the other end and they have a tug of war.)*

BAYLOR: *(Pulling on blanket)* No more blankets! No more free rides! It's time for you to leave! Let go a' this blanket!

(BAYLOR finally yanks the blanket away from FRANKIE. FRANKIE just sits there, rubbing this hands on his shoulders from the cold. He shivers. His eyes dart around the room, trying to figure out where he is.)

Now get up. Get outa that sofa and reach me my socks.

(FRANKIE just stares at BAYLOR. Keeps rubbing his shoulders, shivering.)

BAYLOR: *(Pointing to his socks)* See the socks?

(FRANKIE stares at the socks but makes no move toward them.)

Do you see 'em or not?

(FRANKIE nods.)

Then pick 'em up for me, would ya and put 'em on my feet. My back's seized up and my wife's abandoned me.

FRANKIE: I—I don't think I can get up. I can't feel my leg anymore.

BAYLOR: My feet are turnin' to ice, here! I need my socks!

FRANKIE: Wrap the blanket around them.

(Pause. BAYLOR considers for a moment, then wraps the blanket around his feet. Pause.)

How's that?

BAYLOR: It's not the same as my socks.

FRANKIE: Well, I'm sorry. I just can't get up.

BAYLOR: Yer not injured that bad.

FRANKIE: *(Sudden recognition)* You're the one who shot me, aren't you?

BAYLOR: Don't go gettin' any fancy notions about suing me. I had every right to shoot you. You were on my land.

FRANKIE: I remember you now.

BAYLOR: You won't get anywhere with that Big City stuff back here, boy. That don't hold water in the back country. There's not a lawyer within six hundred miles a' this place.

FRANKIE: I'm not gonna sue you.

BAYLOR: Last lawyer who tried to come back in here, we cut his nuts off.

FRANKIE: Hey look! Hey! I've got a bullet hole in my leg! All right? I've got a bullet hole clean through my leg! And you did it! And it's not gettin' any better. It's gettin' worse, in fact. So don't try to scare me with this stuff about lawyers, because I'm not buyin' it. I've got a serious injury here!

BAYLOR: Aw, stop complainin', will ya. I've had my belly full a' complaints in this house.

FRANKIE: Look—I don't know why it is but nobody around here will make any effort to try and get me outa here. How come that is? My brother—I've got a brother with a real short fuse. He gets weird ideas in his head. It doesn't take much to tip him over the edge. Now I've been here way too long. Way, way past the time I was supposed to get back. And he's gonna start gettin' the wrong idea about me and your daughter. I mean, your daughter is his wife. You know that, don't ya? I mean I suppose you know that but it's hard to tell anymore if anybody knows anything about anybody else around here. Like her, for instance. Your daughter. She is getting very strange with me. Very strange. I mean she started talkin' to me like I was him. Like I was my brother. To her, I mean. Like she thought I was him and not me. Your daughter. Beth. I mean I don't even know if she knows who I am anymore but—she thinks—she thinks her brother—your son and you, in fact—even you—she includes you in this too—she thinks you and him, your son and you, are somehow responsible for taking her brain out. For removing her brain. Did you know about all this?

BAYLOR: Nope.

FRANKIE: No. See? See, that's what I mean. Nobody knows. Nobody seems to know. Nobody seems to have the slightest idea about what's goin on. And meanwhile—MEANWHILE—I AM STUCK HERE TRYING TO GET BACK HOME! AND NOBODY IS MAKING ANY EFFORT TO HELP ME!

BAYLOR: Aw, pipe down, will ya for Christ's sake! Jesus God Almighty! You're worse than all the women in this house put together.

FRANKIE: If I die on you here—If I die, you're gonna be in big trouble, mister. You and everybody else in this family.

BAYLOR: Don't threaten me in my own house! Don't you try and threaten me in my own goddamn house! This isn't Southern California. This is Montana, buster!

(MEG appears again up left in same costume.)

MEG: *(Soft)* Baylor?

BAYLOR: *(Pause, turns to her, leans back in chair)* What is it now?

MEG: Beth's coming down. She wants to talk to you.

(FRANKIE suddenly reaches out for the blanket and jerks it off BAYLOR's feet, wraps it around himself. BAYLOR tries to grab it back but he's too late.)

BAYLOR: Gimme that blanket back! Give it back! That doesn't belong to you.

(FRANKIE keeps blanket, wraps it tightly around himself so he's covered completely with just his head sticking out. Like a mummy.)

MEG: She's coming down here now, Baylor.

BAYLOR: Let her come, for Christ's sake! What in the world is the big fuss all about? She lives in this house. *(Turns back to FRANKIE.)* Gimme back that blanket!

(In the course of this last rant by BAYLOR, BETH *appears beside* MEG *but* BAYLOR *doesn't notice her.* FRANKIE *sees her and tightens his blanket around his shoulders.* BETH *is dressed in a bizarre combination of clothing. She wears black high heels with short woolen bobby socks, a tight pink skirt—below the knee, straight out of the fifties—a fuzzy turquoise-blue short-sleeved, low-cut sweater, green tights. She wears lots of charm bracelets and a silver chain around her neck with a St. Christopher medal, a gold cross and a rabbit's foot.*

She has various kinds of snap earrings encircling her left ear. Her hair is piled high with a small white ribbon tied in a bow at the top. Her face is heavily made up with thick glossy pink lipstick, blue mascara and dark, outlined eyebrows. MEG *takes her hand as she enters and* BETH *just stands there holding hands with her mother. After pause,* BAYLOR *still hasn't seen her.)*

BETH: *(Soft)* Daddy?

*(*BAYLOR *turns to* BETH. *No reaction. Just stares at her for a while.)*

(To MEG*)* Who's this?

BETH: Daddy, I wanna ask you somethin' special.

BAYLOR: *(Another pause, staring at* BETH*)* What in the sam-hell have you got on? What is that getup!

BETH: I wanna get married, Dad.

BAYLOR: You go upstairs right now and take that crap off a' you! Take it all off and go jump in the shower. You look like a roadhouse chippie.

(Pause. BETH *lets go of* MEG's *hand and crosses slowly over to* FRANKIE. FRANKIE *recoils on the sofa, wrapped tightly in the blanket.* BETH *stops in front of him and stares at him.* MEG *stays where she is.* BAYLOR *stays in chair.)*

MEG: Baylor, she's been tryin' for hours to get up the courage enough to come down here and ask you. You don't have to be so hard.

BAYLOR: Beth, are you hearin' what I said?

BETH: *(Staring at* FRANKIE*)* This is my man. This is the one. We're gonna get married, Daddy. I've decided.

BAYLOR: You're already married to one idiot!

(Sudden sound of shot from deer rifle in distance. Immediately on sound of shot, both FRANKIE *and* BAYLOR *stand with a jolt.* FRANKIE *stands straight up on sofa, still keeping the blanket wrapped around him, supporting himself on his bad leg by holding on to back of sofa.* BAYLOR *supports himself by holding arm of chair. They both stare in direction of sound out toward porch.* BETH *keeps staring at* FRANKIE. MEG *and* BETH *pay no attention to the gunshot.)*

BAYLOR: *(Referring to* MIKE*)* He's got another one. How d'ya' like that. I sit out there for weeks on end, freezin' my tail off and come up empty. He gets two in one day. Life is not fair.

*(*MEG *moves slowly toward* BAYLOR.*)*

MEG: Maybe we could have the wedding here, Baylor. That would be nice, wouldn't it? Soon as the weather thaws.

FRANKIE: *(To* MEG*)* She's married to my brother! She's already married! You were there at the wedding. Don't you remember?

MEG: *(To* BAYLOR*)* We could have it up on the high meadow. That would be beautiful. Just like the old times.

FRANKIE: I AM NOT GETTIN' MARRIED TO MY BROTHER'S WIFE!

*(*MIKE *comes running up porch steps into house carrying deer rifle.)*

MIKE: *(As he enters)* I got him! I got him! He's right out there in the shed. I got him good. He's right out there now. He's not goin' anywhere. He walked right into it. Right smack dab into it.

*(*MIKE *crosses slowly over to* FRANKIE, *who remains standing on sofa.* BAYLOR *sits slowly back down in armchair.)*

BAYLOR: *(Sitting)* Well, I'm not dressin' this one out for you. Not me. You can have the pleasure your own self. You think it's so damn smart to go around shootin' game without doin' the labor. It's time you put two and two together, boy.

MIKE: *(To* FRANKIE*)* Guess who I got tied to the stove? He's out there, snivelin' like a baby.

FRANKIE: Jake?

MIKE: *(Goes to* BETH*)* He's gonna apologize to you, Beth. He's gonna make a full apology. Anytime you're ready. He promised me.

BETH: Can you come to the wedding too, Mike? I want everybody to be there. I want the whole family there.

MIKE: *(Moving to* MEG*)* He's gonna apologize to all of us. You too, Mom.

MEG: Who is it? Nobody has to apologize to me. Nobody has ever offended me in any way.

MIKE: *(Moving to* BAYLOR*)* He's already begging. I got him beggin'. He's on his knees out there, Dad.

FRANKIE: You didn't shoot him too, did you? What're you tryin' to do? Kill my whole family off?

MIKE: *(Moving to* FRANKIE*)* I didn't have to shoot him. I just scared him. Soon as he saw me, he broke down.

BAYLOR: What'd you do with that rack? I want that rack! It belongs to me. I'm gonna put that rack on the wall.

MIKE: It's out there too. It's all out there. We can all go out and visit him. One at a time. He'll confess to us. I broke him down good. You shoulda seen him. He was crawlin'. I just kept him on his knees. I kept him there. You shoulda seen it, Dad. Every time he'd try to stand up, I'd knock him back down. Just hammer him down until he gave up completely. He gave himself up to me. He's my prisoner now. You wanna see? Just come out on the porch and I'll go back down there and turn him loose. You watch. He'll do anything I say now. I've got him trained.

BAYLOR: I just want the rack. That's all I wanna see.

MIKE: *(Moving toward porch)* I'll go get him. I'll go get him and bring him up here to the house. You won't believe it when you see him. He's not gonna bother any of us again. I guarantee ya that.

(MIKE exits. Pause. They all remain. Silence.)

FRANKIE: Why did it have to snow!

(Suddenly BAYLOR makes a lunge for FRANKIE, grabs hold of the blanket and rips it off FRANKIE. FRANKIE just stands there on the sofa. BAYLOR slowly wraps himself in blanket all the way up to his neck and sits back down in the chair slowly. Pause. Then BETH very softly moves in on FRANKIE, who just stands there, staring off in the direction of MIKE's exit.)

BETH: *(To FRANKIE)* It's all right. Once we're together, the whole world will change. You'll see. We'll be in a whole new world.

(BETH embraces FRANKIE around his waist and puts her head gently on his stomach as FRANKIE remains standing, looking out. Pause. MEG looks at them.)

MEG: I think it would be wonderful up on the high meadow. We could invite the whole family. We could even have a picnic up there. Cake and lemonade. We could have music. We haven't had a real wedding in so long.

(Lights fade . . .)

SCENE 3

Lights up, stage-right set, on LORRAINE *and* SALLY. LORRAINE *is dressed up in a dark suit, white blouse, with a bow around her neck, a dressy hat, high heels and stockings. She lies on top of the bedclothes with her back propped up with pillows, poring through one of several travel brochures. The kind with lots of foldout color photographs of European landscapes. Her purse is slung over one of the bedposts. Two large, open suitcases lie on the floor at the foot of the bed, half packed with clothes.* SALLY's *suitcase is beside the bed, ready to go. The chair is pulled out into the middle of the room surrounded by cardboard boxes full of odd papers and paraphernalia from the men.* SALLY *sits on the chair in a dress and high heels facing audience, picking through the boxes and throwing different items into a large pile of junk—in a metal bucket on the floor in front of her. Included in the pile are all the model airplanes which used to hang over the bed. As lights rise on them, the two women continue their separate activities for a little while,* LORRAINE *avidly looking through the brochures and, every once in a while, making notes with a pen in a small dimestore notebook beside her. She also sips from a cup of coffee.* SALLY *keeps throwing papers into the pile, once in a while reading parts of an old letter to herself, chuckling, then crumpling the paper up and tossing it, then reaching into a box for another one. Now and then she comes across an old photograph, stares at it and throws that away, too. Once this quiet, introverted mood is established,* SALLY *picks out another photo from a box, stares at it, then holds it up for* LORRAINE *to look at.*

SALLY: *(Holding up photo, still sitting)* You wanna save this?

> *(*LORRAINE *lowers the brochure she's involved with and squints toward the photo.)*

LORRAINE: What is it?

SALLY: Picture of you in some parade. I don't know.

LORRAINE: *(Going back to her brochure)* Naw, toss it.

(SALLY *throws photo into pile, digs into another box.)*

LORRAINE: *(Lowers brochure again)* Wait a second. What parade?

SALLY: I don't know. How many were you in?

LORRAINE: Quite a bunch. Lemme see it.

(SALLY *gets up from chair, picks through pile of junk and locates photo
again. She picks it up and takes it over to* LORRAINE.)

SALLY: *(Looking at photo, as she crosses)* Looks like the forties or something.

LORRAINE: *(Taking photo and holding it away from herself, squints at it)*
Lemme see. *(Stares at photo.)* Oh—I know. This was down in
Victorville. Had a big "Frontier Days" blowout there. Big to-do.
That was my sorrel mare.

SALLY: What year was that?

LORRAINE: Musta been 'forty-five, 'forty-six. Right around the end of
the war. Yeah, big barbecue, square dance. The whole fandango.
Pretty little mare, isn't she?

SALLY: Yeah. Were you in a lot of parades?

LORRAINE: Every chance I'd get. Used to just love gettin' out there
with the sequins and jing-a-bobs and all that Spanish music. We
had us a great old time.

SALLY: Dad went too?

LORRAINE: Yeah, he'd ride right alongside me. He had that big dumb
gray gelding you had to throw down on his side every time you
went to reshoe him. Dumb as a post.

SALLY: I didn't know you did all that.

LORRAINE: Oh, yeah. We lived pretty high there for a while.

SALLY: I never knew that. You wanna save this one, then?

LORRAINE: *(Hands photo back to* SALLY*)* Naw, burn it.

SALLY: *(Taking photo)* You sure?

LORRAINE: What do I wanna save it for? It's all in the past. Dead and gone. Just a picture.

*(*LORRAINE *goes back to her brochures as* SALLY *crosses back to pile of junk, holding photo.)*

SALLY: *(Reaching chair, looking at photo)* Okay if I keep it?

LORRAINE: *(Reading brochure)* Fine by me. Don't know what good it's gonna do ya.

SALLY: I just like the picture.

LORRAINE: Sure, go ahead and keep it. That was one heck of a little mare, I'll tell ya. She'd go anywhere, anytime.

SALLY: *(Putting photo in her purse, hanging on the chair)* What ever happened to her?

LORRAINE: She went with the rest of 'em. One day he just decided he was sick a' feedin' livestock and he loaded everything into the trailer and hauled 'em all off someplace. That was the last I saw of her. Probably wound up in a dog dish.

(Pause. SALLY *goes back to rummaging through the boxes, throwing things on the pile.* LORRAINE *studies her brochures.* SALLY *pulls an old letter out of one of the boxes, opens it and starts to read it to herself.)*

SALLY: *(After reading to herself for a while)* Here's a letter from Frankie, right after he won that baseball scholarship.

LORRAINE: I found it. Here it is. Right here. Sligo County. Connaught.

*(*LORRAINE *starts pointing excitedly at a big colorful map of Ireland. She holds it up to show* SALLY*.)*

I'll be darned. There it is, right there.

SALLY: Is that where we're goin'?

LORRAINE: That's it. I've still got some people back there if I can ever track 'em down. Been so long since anybody's ever heard from 'em.

SALLY: What's their names?

LORRAINE: Skellig. Mary Skellig and there was a Shem or Sham or somethin' like that. Shem Skellig, I think it was. Probably her husband.

SALLY: How're we gonna find 'em?

LORRAINE: Oh, those little tiny villages back there. Everybody knows everybody. All we gotta do is ask. They're real friendly folks back there.

SALLY: You've never been there before, have you?

LORRAINE: Nope. But I used to remember my grandma talk about it. She said they were all real friendly. We shouldn't have much trouble.

(SALLY *continues going through the boxes and tossing things out as they talk.*)

SALLY: Did you talk to a travel agent about this?

LORRAINE: They gave me all this stuff down at the Irish Embassy, or whatever you call it. That building with the green flag in the window. It's not gonna be a problem. All we gotta do is get there and ask around.

(LORRAINE *is now poring through a book and some other pamphlets as she keeps referring back to the map of Ireland. Pause.*)

SALLY: What happens when we do find them?

LORRAINE: Whad'ya mean?

SALLY: I mean, if you haven't had any contact with them for so long, maybe they won't even know who we are.

LORRAINE: They'll know. All I gotta do is tell 'em my maiden name and they'll remember.

SALLY: Are we gonna live with them?

LORRAINE: No, no. We'll just stay for a little visit. Save on motel bills.

(Pause as they continue their respective activities.)

SALLY: Who are these people?

LORRAINE: What people?

SALLY: The uh—Skelligs.

LORRAINE: Relatives. Ancestors. I don't know.

SALLY: Maybe they're all dead.

LORRAINE: People don't just all die. They don't just all up and die at once unless it's a catastrophe or somethin'. Someone's always left behind to carry on. There's always at least one straggler left behind. Now we'll just ask around until we find out who that is. We'll track him down. And then we'll introduce ourselves. It's not gonna be that difficult a task.

(Pause. They continue activities. SALLY *pulls out a blue rosette ribbon, slightly faded, won at some livestock show. She holds it up for* LORRAINE *to see, then tosses it into bucket.)*

SALLY: *(Standing behind pile of junk and boxes)* How're we gonna haul all this junk outa here, Mom?

LORRAINE: We're not gonna haul it. We're gonna burn it.

SALLY: I know, but we've gotta get it outa the house somehow.

LORRAINE: What for?

SALLY: Well, what're we gonna do, burn the house down?

LORRAINE: Why not?

(Pause. SALLY *stares at* LORRAINE.*)*

SALLY: We're gonna burn the whole house down?

LORRAINE: That's right. The whole slam bang. Oughta make a pretty nice light, don't ya think? Little show for the neighbors.

(SALLY *starts to laugh.*)

What's so damn funny?

(SALLY *stops laughing.*)

SALLY: How're we gonna do it?

LORRAINE: Well, ya light one a' them Blue Diamond stick matches and toss it in there and run. That's the way I always did it.

SALLY: You mean we're just gonna run away and let it burn?

(LORRAINE *picks up a box of wooden matches and approaches the pail of junk.*)

LORRAINE: Nah—maybe we won't run. Maybe we'll just stand out there on the front lawn, the two of us, and watch it burn for a while. Sing a song maybe. Do a little jig. Then we'll just turn and walk away. Just walk.

SALLY: Well, we're not gonna have any place to come back to, Mom.

LORRAINE: Who's comin' back?

(*Lights dim slowly as* LORRAINE *strikes a match and lights the pile of papers in the bucket. The fire in the bucket keeps glowing. Simultaneously, lights are rising center stage. From deep upstage center,* JAKE *emerges into the light, walking on his knees straight toward the audience with the American flag between his teeth and stretched taut on either side of his head, like a set of driving reins for a draft horse. Behind* JAKE, *holding an end of the flag in each hand,* MIKE *walks along, clucking to* JAKE *like a horse and shaking the "reins" now and then. The deer rifle is tucked under* MIKE's *arm. They continue this way with* MIKE *driving* JAKE *downstage center. Lights reach their peak.* MIKE *reins* JAKE *in to a stop.* JAKE *remains on his knees. Fire keeps burning in bucket stage right.*)

MIKE: *(Pulling back on flag)* Ho! Ho, now!

(JAKE *stops.*)

That's it.

(JAKE *stays in one place on his knees as* MIKE *comes up beside him and takes the flag out of his mouth and rolls it up in a ball around his rifle. Now and then, he pats* JAKE *on the head, as he would an old horse.*

JAKE *is silent. He has deep bruises around his eyes and jaw. His knees are bleeding and the knuckles on both hands. He's in same costume as at end of Act II.*)

MIKE: *(Removing flag, patting* JAKE*)* Atta boy. You're gonna do just fine. Pretty soon we can take you right out into the woods. Drag some timber. You'll like that. *(Rolling flag up around the rifle.)* Now, I want you to stay right here. You understand?

(JAKE *nods his head.*)

I don't want you wanderin' off. I want you to wait right here for me. I'm gonna go inside and get Beth. You remember her, don't ya?

(JAKE *nods.*)

You remember what you're gonna say to her?

(JAKE *nods.*)

You're not gonna forget?

(JAKE *shakes his head.*)

You're gonna tell her everything that we talked about, aren't ya?

(JAKE *nods.*)

Good. And you're not gonna touch her. You're not gonna even think about gettin' close to her.

(JAKE shakes his head.)

Good. Now, just stay right here and wait for me. Don't move an inch.

(JAKE remains on his knees, staring out toward audience. MIKE crosses with rifle wrapped in flag, toward stage-left set. Lights rise on set as MIKE moves toward it. BAYLOR is asleep in chair with blanket wrapped tight around him. Only his head and feet stick out. MEG is absent. BETH, in same costume as at e.. of Scene 2, Act III, is tucking the throw rug from the floor around FRANKIE, who lies on his back, shivering violently on the sofa, head upstage, staring at ceiling. Light remains up on JAKE. MIKE walks up the porch steps and onto landing. He stops there and speaks to BETH, who remains involved with FRANKIE.)

MIKE: He's ready now, Beth. You can come outside and he'll apologize to you. You just stay on the porch with me. He won't come near you.

BETH: *(Referring to FRANKIE)* He's shaking all over. I don't think he's getting any better, Mike. We can't keep him here. Maybe we could get married in the hospital.

MIKE: Beth! Forget about him now. Okay? I want you to come out here and listen to what your husband's got to say. I went to a lot a' trouble gettin' him to come around to my way a' thinkin'.

(Pause. BETH turns to MIKE.)

BETH: Who's out there?

MIKE: Jake!! The one you've been askin' about all this time. The one you couldn't live without. Your old pal, Jake! He's right outside there and he wants to tell you something.

BETH: He's dead.

(Pause. MIKE *stares at her.)*

MIKE: All right.

*(*MIKE *makes a sudden, violent move toward her and grabs her by the arm. He starts to drag her toward the porch.* BETH *resists.)*

BETH: DADDY! HE'S TRYING TO TAKE ME AWAY! DADDY!

*(*BAYLOR *suddenly wakes up and stands abruptly. The blanket falls to his feet.)*

BAYLOR: *(To* MIKE*)* What's goin' on here?

BETH: He's trying to take me outside. I don't wanna go outside now.

*(*BETH *pulls away from* MIKE *and runs back to* FRANKIE. *She kneels beside him by the sofa and strokes his head.* BAYLOR *seems totally disoriented for a moment, then focuses on* MIKE's *rifle with the flag wrapped around it.)*

MIKE: Beth, you get back here!

BAYLOR: *(Referring to rifle)* What're you doin' with that?

MIKE: Dad, I've got the bastard right outside on his knees. He's agreed to make an apology to the whole family. Where's Mom?

BAYLOR: Never mind that. What're you doin' with that rifle? What's that wrapped around it?

MIKE: It's just a flag. He had it on him. He had it all wrapped around him. I wanted Beth to come out so he could—

BAYLOR: *(Pause. Taking a step toward* MIKE, *kicking blanket away)* It's not just a flag. That's the flag of our nation. Isn't that the flag of our nation wrapped around that rifle?

MIKE: Yeah, I guess so. I don't know. I'm tryin' to tell you somethin' here. The flag's not the issue!

BAYLOR: You don't know? You don't recognize the flag anymore? It's the same color it always was. They haven't changed it, have they? Maybe added a star or two but otherwise it's exactly the same. How could you not recognize it?

(BAYLOR is slowly moving in on MIKE, who backs up slightly as he approaches, keeping the rifle pointed low.)

MIKE: Dad, I'm tryin' to tell you that I've got him turned around. I've got him totally convinced that he was wrong. He wants to confess to all of us. He owes it to us.

BAYLOR: Don't let that flag touch the ground!

(MIKE quickly raises the rifle so it's pointed directly at BAYLOR but only accidentally. MIKE is still backing up as BAYLOR moves slowly toward him.)

Don't point it at me! What's the matter with you! Have you lost your mind?

(MIKE quickly raises the rifle over his head.)

MIKE: I've got Jake out there on his knees. The guy who beat up your daughter!

BAYLOR: Gimme that flag! Hand it over to me! Hand it over.

(MIKE lowers the rifle, takes the flag off it and hands it to BAYLOR. BAYLOR snatches it out of his hands. BETH goes to the blanket unnoticed by BAYLOR and takes it back to FRANKIE, covering him with it tightly like a mummy.)

BAYLOR: *(Folding the flag up and tucking it under his arm)* What do ya think yer doin', using the American flag like a grease rag. Gimme that rifle.

MIKE: Dad—

BAYLOR: Gimme that rifle!

(MIKE hands the rifle over to BAYLOR.)

Haven't you got anything better to do than to monkey around with weapons and flags? Go outside and make yerself useful.

(BAYLOR turns away from MIKE and heads back for his chair with the rifle and flag. Pause.)

MIKE: So it doesn't make any difference, is that it? None of it makes any difference? My sister can get her brains knocked out and it doesn't make a goddamn bit a' difference to anyone in this family! All you care about is a flag? *(He points out toward JAKE.)*

It was him who was wearin' it! He's the traitor, not me! I'm the one who's loyal to this family! I'm the only one.

BAYLOR: *(Approaching chair, disoriented)* What's happened to my blanket now?

MIKE: Doesn't anybody recognize that we've been betrayed? From the inside out. He married into this family and he deceived us all. He deceived her! He lied to her! He told her he loved her!

(Short pause as BAYLOR stands by the chair searching for his blanket, still with flag, oblivious to everything else.)

BAYLOR: *(Looking behind chair for blanket)* How do things disappear around here?

(MIKE suddenly bursts across the set and picks up BETH in his arms. She clings to the blanket and as MIKE tears her away from FRANKIE, she drags the blanket with her. BAYLOR pays no attention.)

BETH: *(Being dragged away by MIKE)* NOOOOOOOOOO!!!!

(MIKE carries BETH across the set to the porch and down the steps to JAKE, who remains on his knees facing audience. He sets BETH down on her feet, facing JAKE, and forces her to look at JAKE.)

MIKE: *(Holding BETH in place)* Now look at him! Look at him! Isn't that the man you love? Isn't that him? Isn't that the one you say is dead?

(BETH *shakes her head.*)

MIKE: *(Shaking her by the shoulders)* Look at him! *(To* JAKE*)* Get up on your feet. Stand up!

*(*MIKE *grabs* JAKE *by the collar still holding on to* BETH. JAKE *struggles to stand.)*

Get up on your feet and tell her what you're gonna say. Tell her everything we talked about in the shed. Go ahead and tell her now. Go ahead!

(Pause as JAKE *stands there, trying to maintain a vertical position. He stares at* BETH. *He tries to form the words but falters on them.)*

JAKE: *(Softly)* I—I—I—I love you more than this earth.

(Pause. Then MIKE *lets go of* BETH *and grabs* JAKE *by the shoulders. Shakes him.* JAKE *offers no resistance.)*

MIKE: *(Shaking* JAKE*)* That's not what you were gonna say! Tell her what you were gonna say! We had it all memorized!

*(*BETH *suddenly runs back up the steps, still holding on to the blanket, and enters the set again. She stops and stares at* BAYLOR. FRANKIE *rolls toward her on the sofa.)*

MIKE: *(Staying with* JAKE*)* BETH!!

BAYLOR: *(To* BETH*)* What're you doin' with that blanket?

BETH: *(Looking at* FRANKIE*)* I was gonna—I wanted to keep him warm.

BAYLOR: *(Moving to* BETH*)* Gimme that blanket.

*(*BAYLOR *snatches the blanket out of* BETH's *hand and heads for the chair. He tosses the blanket on the chair but keeps hold of the flag.* BETH *stays where she is.)*

BETH: *(As* BAYLOR *moves away from her)* Daddy—

(BETH *stays marooned in one spot with her back to* JAKE *and* MIKE, *facing* FRANKIE *and* BAYLOR. BAYLOR *starts to try to fold the flag up but makes a mess of it.)*

Daddy, there's a man—

(MIKE *turns* JAKE *facing into the stage-left set.)*

MIKE: *(Behind* JAKE, *hands on his shoulders, whispers in his ear)* Look! Look in there. You see them? You can go right on in there now. They won't mind. They won't even notice. They won't even know you're an enemy. Your brother's in there, too. See him in there? He's with her now. He's with Beth. They've been sleeping together ever since he got here. I'll bet you didn't know that, did ya? They've been sleeping together right there on that sofa. Nobody cares, see. Dad doesn't care. Mom doesn't. Nobody cares. They've just all lost track of things. Go on in there and introduce yourself. I'll bet they take you right into the family. You could use a family, couldn't ya? You look like you could use a family. Well, that's good, see. That's good. Because, they could use a son. A son like you. Go ahead.

(MIKE *pats* JAKE *on the back, and exits upstage into darkness, leaving* JAKE *at the bottom of the porch steps facing into the stage-left set.* MEG *enters from up-left door.)*

MEG: Isn't anyone coming to bed? It's nighttime, isn't it?

BAYLOR: Meg, come here and help me fold this flag. You remember how to fold a flag, don't ya?

(BETH *takes a few steps toward* MEG, *but it's as though she's isolated in her own world now. Neither* MEG *nor* BAYLOR *recognizes her presence.)*

BETH: *(Moving toward* MEG, *then stopping again)* Mom—

MEG: *(Moving to* BAYLOR*)* I'm not sure. Did I ever fold one before?

(JAKE *starts to move slowly up the steps and onto the landing.* FRANKIE *sees him now from the sofa.* BETH *still has her back toward* JAKE. BAYLOR *has handed one end of the flag to* MEG *as they back away from each other upstage, stretching the flag out between them.*)

BAYLOR: *(To* MEG*)* Don't let it touch the ground now. Just back away from me and we'll stretch it out first. Don't let it touch the ground whatever you do.

MEG: I won't.

(JAKE *keeps moving slowly, from the porch right into the set.* FRANKIE *props himself up on the sofa, staring at him.*)

FRANKIE: Jake?

(BETH *whirls around fast and sees* JAKE. *Their eyes lock.* BETH *stays where she is.* JAKE *keeps moving.*)

I been tryin' to get ahold of you, Jake. I've been stuck here. For days. I couldn't get out.

BETH: *(Eyes still on* JAKE*)* Daddy, there's a man here. There's a man here now.

BAYLOR: *(With flag)* Now there's a right way to do this and a wrong way, Meg. I want you to pay attention.

MEG: I am.

BAYLOR: It's important.

BETH: THERE'S A MAN IN HERE! HE'S IN OUR HOUSE!

(BAYLOR *and* MEG *pay no attention to the others but continue with the flag.* JAKE *now inside the stage-left set, stops and stares at* BETH. *They keep their eyes on each other. Pause. He takes a step toward her, then stops.*)

JAKE: *(To* BETH, *very simple)* These things—in my head—lie to me. Everything lies. Tells me a story. Everything in me lies. But you.

You stay. You are true. I know you now. You are true. I love you more than this life. You stay. You stay with him. He's my brother.

(JAKE *moves to chair and picks the blanket up. He wraps himself up in it around his shoulders.* FRANKIE *struggles to sit up on sofa.* BETH *stays close to him.*)

FRANKIE: Jake! Wait a second. Jake! What're you doin'?

(JAKE *moves to* BETH, *wrapped in blanket.* BETH *pulls back away from* JAKE.)

BETH: I remember now. The first time I saw you. The very first time I ever saw you. Do you remember that too?

JAKE: *(To* BETH*)* Just one kiss. Just one.

(*Slowly* JAKE *leans toward* BETH *and kisses her softly on the forehead. She lets him, then pulls back to* FRANKIE. JAKE *smiles at her, then turns and exits across stage right, toward porch, with blanket.* FRANKIE *struggles to stand with* BETH *holding on to him.*)

FRANKIE: *(To* JAKE *as he exits)* JAKE!! Jake, you gotta take her with you!! It's not true, Jake! She belongs to you! You gotta take her with you! I never betrayed you! I was true to you!

(JAKE *moves down the porch steps and exits upstage into darkness. He never looks back.* BETH *very softly embraces* FRANKIE *and lays her head on his chest. They remain there in the embrace as* MEG *and* BAYLOR *continue with their flag folding.*)

BAYLOR: *(Folding flag with* MEG*)* Now, the stars have to end up on the outside. I remember that much. Who's got the stars?

MEG: I do.

BAYLOR: Okay. Then I've gotta fold toward you. In little triangles. You just stay put.

(BAYLOR folds the flag in triangles, military-style, toward MEG, who stays where she is, holding the other end.)

Now if everything works out right we should have all the stars on the outside and all the stripes tucked in.

MEG: Why do they do it like that?

BAYLOR: I don't know. Just tradition I guess. That's the way I was taught. Funny how things come back to ya' after all those years.

(BAYLOR finishes the last fold and holds the flag up.)

There! Look at that! We did it! We did it, Meg!

(BAYLOR picks MEG up and twirls her around, then sets her down and kisses her on the cheek, holding flag up.)

I'll be gall-darned if we didn't do it. It's letter perfect. Looks like right outa the manual.

(MEG holds her hand to her cheek where BAYLOR kissed her. She steps back away from him and stares around the room, bewildered. She doesn't notice FRANKIE and BETH.)

What'sa matter?

MEG: I believe that's the first time you've kissed me in twenty years.

BAYLOR: Aw, come on, it ain't been that long. Let's go on up to bed now.

(Pause as BAYLOR looks at MEG. She turns and stares out toward porch, keeping her hand to her cheek.)

Meg?

MEG: I'll be up in a while.

BAYLOR: Well, I'm goin' up. You shut the lights when you come. And don't dawdle. I don't wanna get woke up in the middle of a good dream.

(BAYLOR exits up-left door with flag. Pause. MEG *moves slowly down right toward porch, still unaware of* BETH *and* FRANKIE. *She stares out across the stage to the fire still burning in the bucket. She moves out onto porch landing and stares into space. She stops. Pause.)*

MEG: *(Still with hand to her cheek)* Looks like a fire in the snow. How could that be?

(Lights fade slowly to black except for fire.)